Roots and Ties

Roots and Ties

A Scrapbook of Northeast Memories

GENNY ZAK KIELEY

NODIN PRESS

ISBN: 0931714-95-8

Nodin Press, a division of Micawber's, Inc.
530 North Third Street Suite 120
Minneapolis, MN 55401

This book is dedicated to all the people of Northeast
Who value the past
But also believe in the promise of the future.
And to those who have made Northeast what it is
A VERY SPECIAL PLACE

"Connections between successive generations
of Americans concretely linking their ways of life—are broken by demolition.
Sources of memory cease to exist. We need old buildings in the sun
to gauge our humaneness against indifferent skies."

With Heritage So Rich
U.S. Conference of Mayors
Special Commission on Historic Preservation

Acknowledgments

Thank you to all those who helped make my journey such a pleasant and memorable experience! To those who went out of their way to gather photos and encouraged others to do so too: George Belair, Audrey Ringdol, Jim Dusenka, and Phyllis Askay, I am grateful for your effort. A special thanks to Corinne Diffley, Margaret Hoben and Alice Rainville for sharing their memories for the parochial school section. And to those who allowed me to use their life stories: Jim Cornish, Jim Higgins, and Cindy Spears for providing me with information on Leo and Edward Zaworski. A big thanks to those who helped with the Rhythmland section including Caroline Gage, Nancy O'Dette and Shelly Halford.

To my publisher, Norton Stillman thanks for believing in me. I would like to give recognition to Ruth Jurisch and LuAnn Golen for their diligent work and for going beyond the call of duty to get just the right photos. To my Writers Group a great big hug: Judy Granahan, Dave Hannula, Ruth Jurisch, Lyn LaCoursiere, Joannie Moses, Christina Potyondy, Mona Smith and Ross Tarantino. These are people who I have learned to depend on for so many things. They generously read and made comments on various sections of the book. I would be lost without their ideas, editing, and encouragement.

Most of all I am grateful to my family who are always there for me with vital help and encouragement: Joe, Melanie, DJ, Anthony and Andy. They handed out flyers on hot muggy days, ran errands, sold books, and gave support whenever I needed it. I love you guys. To my husband Doug, who is my editor (yes, he's good at it), photographer, book carrier and everything in between, my loving thanks. I couldn't do it without you.

Contents

Foreword

It all started one day in 1991 as I was driving down Lowry Avenue, I saw a few boarded-up businesses and found myself crying softly. I wondered who would remember how these boarded-up storefronts were back when they were filled with energy and bustling with people? And I wondered who would tell the stories of the way things were? I began to fear the stories would be lost as people got older, and many were already gone.

I don't know if I was the most likely candidate to write the history of Northeast Minneapolis. After all, I wasn't even born Northeast. I came to Minneapolis from a farm in Harding, Minnesota when I was six years old. I came to love this place where teachers and storekeepers gave smiles and encouragement to a lonely little girl. But I did have my own qualifications-a love of history, a love of Northeast, and my own determination to preserve memories.

I began my books on Northeast as a search of information, mostly for my own family. I wanted my kids to know what it was like to grow up in a place like Northeast Minneapolis. But things were changing. The little neighborhood stores where the owner lived in the back were disappearing. In fact, most of the storefront buildings that were so common in Northeast were sitting empty and some were even boarded up. My old school was gone. All the theaters in Northeast were closed. The busy bus routes like Second Street were no longer main thoroughfares.

Just since the beginning of researching my first book in 1993 there had been so many changes. The Shoreham Yard Soo Shops building on Central Avenue has been torn down. One day it just wasn't there anymore, a building that was a part of my life for more than forty years. The last drugstore-Dady's Second Street Pharmacy, a place where we hung out almost every night when I went to Sheridan Junior High, closed in 1997. Another institution in Northeast was gone. Once again my heart broke.

But along with the closing of a lot of favorite places there has also been a rebirth to Northeast Minneapolis. Central Avenue, the commercial heart of Northeast is making a comeback. A cleanup is underway which has included both the removing of false fronts to expose original exterior and the revamping of unsightly alleys. Twenty years ago Central Avenue was a major business district and community that had strong ties to the neighborhood. Business owners are adding a new face to the once seedy business district and brightening it up by installing new trees, lighting, awnings, planters and restored storefronts. There slogan is "Keep Northeast Beautiful."

East Hennepin has undergone a remarkable transformation too. This area was once a thriving business district in the 1960s, almost as popular as Downtown or the Dales Shopping Centers of today. More recently it became filled with boarded up storefronts and skidrow riffraff that hung out on the side walk. It is now a combination of expensive houses, trendy bars and restaurants. The neighborhood has gone from being an ethnic community where people worked in local factories, mills and railroads to a more diverse community of professionals. Since the 1980s hundreds of new housing units have been built.

One of the most exciting changes in Northeast is the community of artists who have moved in and taken over the old unused vacant business buildings. Three of the largest buildings are the Thorpe Building, Northrup King, and the California Building. The neighborhood is renewing itself. And new families and young people are moving in and loving it.

My collection that I started in 1993 of "Things Northeast" combined with interviews of people's memories and wonderful old and sometimes rare photographs became my first book, Heart and Hard Work: Memories of Nordeast Minneapolis, it was published by Nodin Press in December of 1997. Two years later, in December of 1999, Nodin published my second book, Pride and Tradition: More Memories of Northeast Minneapolis.

I've learned more in the years of researching and writing these books, and have met more people than I ever knew when I was growing up Northeast. I know more about the different ethnic groups now. After all, I grew up on a block where almost everyone was Polish. But there is a basic common thread among Northeasters. There is a saying that if you know one person from Northeast you know several because they're all connected by this invisible grapevine.

The people of Northeast are hard working, honest, not pretentious, and they also like to have a good time. There are more get togethers and church festivals here than any other part of the city. They are lovers of history and good story tellers. They love to have reunions and talk about the old days. One group from Mike's Bar of about 75 people, still has reunions even though the bar closed in 1960. They are proud of their heritage, and like to hold onto traditions. And they are still that way, even amidst all the changes.

After my two books came out what struck me most about the phone calls and the letters I received from people all over the country was the yearning of "ordinary people to have their lives recorded and valued. "You've told my story," they said. And they were delighted that someone thought their lives were worth writing about.

People whom I had forgotten about appeared as if out of a time warp. My third grade teacher, Mrs. Remquist, showed up at a booksigning. She had a special pride in one of her students writing a book about Northeast.

The comments have warmed my heart. Sometimes I heard from strangers who felt as though they knew me. "Thank you for helping me understand my mother." "You made my dad cry." "My mother has only read two things in her life, and one of them was your book."

One lady said she loved the book but it was too heavy for her to read in the bathtub. And then there was the man whose last request was to have my book put in the casket with him.

We owe a great deal to the savers, the picture takers, and those who hunt down information. They are the keepers of the culture that has been handed down through the generations, telling the stories that were told at gatherings, at the dinner table, while baking cookies or bread with Grandma, while working in the garden, canning tomatoes, or making jam. "My mother used to do it this way. . . ." "My father used to hitch up the horse to pull us on the sled to school." I loved those old stories. I just couldn't get enough of them.

Our family stories are filled with pain and joy. And these stories are passed down from parent to child to grandchild through the generations, so that the experiences will not be forgotten. These stories must be told so that those who come after us will know how it really was. You and I are the only ones who can tell them.

—Genny Zak Kieley

Grandma and Grandpa's trunk that came from Poland in 1903.

1 Treasures in the Attic

It wasn't until June of 1983, shortly after the Sears home improvement guys came to insulate the attic and left debris all over the floor that my interest in my heritage fully bloomed. The chaos the workman had left and the loose insulation bothered my mother so much that every time I visited her, she mentioned what a mess the attic was. So out of duty I drove to her house dressed in grubby clothes, determined to do my finest job of cleaning. As I pulled up I could see the two-story stucco house with the porch that was lined with windows all the way across the front. How often I'd sat in that porch on summer afternoons playing dolls with the neighborhood girls.

Mom and Doxie 1970s.

My mother and her dog, Doxie greeted me at the door. She was dressed in a flowered housedress and a red checked apron. Strands of soft white hair that had been once a golden red were now pulled back into a barrette at the back of her head. And her blue gray eyes were smiling. Living alone for the last five years, her fearless companion, Doxie with his high-pitched bark had frightened away possible intruders, as well as a few harmless mailmen. After he licked my feet for a while he realized I was not a stranger. We walked through her living room where African Violets were blooming in the front window all arranged on a black metal plant stand. The familiar smell of lilacs, which were carefully placed in a glass vase on the dining room table and Moms cooking wafted over me as I walked through the house. We greeted each other at the door and went through to the kitchen. Doxie lay down to rest while my mother and I sat down at the gray and pink Formica table.

I looked around the room. The Polish Blessing plaque hung against a wall of red checked wallpaper and a picture of the Last Supper hung beside the plastic clock that ticked loudly. A red and yellow ceramic rooster stood on top of my mother's archaic white gas stove. A farmhouse sink was in the middle of the room. Even though it was 1983 she was still using a wringer wash machine and lighting her oven with a match.

Mom in her kitchen 1980s.

For some reason the familiar things that had just seemed old in the past were quaint and comforting to me today. In my ever-changing world, I could count on the continuity of this house, and of my roots.

"Let's not have coffee. I'm anxious to get started," I said knowing the suggestion was useless. So I prepared myself for mom's strong coffee that was always the color of dark brown mud. In her conservative upbringing she often reused the coffee grounds. "Here, have a

cinnamon roll," she said as I went into the pantry to grab a cup.

"I've already eaten, Mom."

The pantry had shelves that were lined with flowered Contac paper and a table that my grandfather made. Canned goods, staples and silverware were on one side. On the other side were larger shelves with a few of my grandma's old fashioned turquoise pottery dishes, large platters and a hand made cutting board shaped like a pig. There was a ton of pink melmac dishes and the glassware and plates that my mother had collected over the years, "Give aways" from gas stations and boxes of laundry detergent. Who knows what was on that top shelf? Maybe that free glass pitcher that she received for buying twelve bars of Camay soap in all different colors. Or the thermal basket weave cups and bowls that she got at the dimestore.

Inside the pantry she kept a small metal linen closet with pink flowered decals on the doors. All the linens and the new towels that she rarely used were kept in there. My mother's motto was to save everything for good—for Sundays and holidays. To this day I still have trouble forcing myself to use a new dishtowel.

"How are the kids?" she asked.

"They're busy with school activities, I don't see them so much anymore." When we finished our coffee Mom handed me a broom. We headed for the backporch and walked up the rickety stairs with no railing. The backporch was a kind of mudroom where paint and tools were stored. My mother called it "the Shinya," which is Polish for back porch. It was an older part of the house that had been made of boxcar lumber. Rough boards along the back wall were carved with my uncles' and their friends' initials. Underneath the stairs was a trapdoor that lead to the basement. At the top of the stairs there was a small landing with flowered linoleum tacked down. The back porch was added on later. Because of that there were two doors at the top of the stairs. This always seemed strange to me, this extra doorway that you couldn't get to.

As we headed up the stairs she let me take her hand. Suddenly I experienced the role reversal where I became the parent. When we got to the top she stepped in front of me, "I haven't been up here in a long time." She turned the doorknob. Nothing happened.

"Allow me, " I said. I set one shoulder against the door and grabbed onto the handle, pushing as hard as I could. I almost flew into the room.

She laughed and grabbed my hand. "Be careful, you could have hurt yourself."

As soon as we were in, the steaming air rushed toward us. Then all this junk sprang into view. Trunks and suitcases, a huge pile of magazines, kitchen chairs without seats, and an outdated electric fan. In one corner a sprawling, high heap of discarded shoes, open toed high heels next to old work boots. On top of the heap a home made wooden guitar and an old washboard.

"What are we going to do with it all?" I asked as I maneuvered past a standing metal ashtray and a box filled with rolls of old wallpaper. One of the three rooms was filled entirely with boxes that were jammed with old Christmas ornaments, plastic flowers, and yellowed photographs that were brimming over. Mixed in were sheets of used wrapping paper and newspaper clippings.

"You have birth, marriage and death announcements of everyone you've ever known. Who are these people anyway?"

"Neighbors, friends and relatives."

I laughed, "Didn't you ever throw anything away?"

"I just recorded life. Kept track of it all. These are like my diaries," she said." I told you it was a mess. Now it's become a dumping grounds."

My brother John's First Communion 1930s.

My brother Bob's wedding to Ceil 1952.

"Don't worry, " I said. Then I sneezed a couple of times from the dust. We started sorting things into three piles—one for the Goodwill, one for throw away and one for keeping. Then we moved all the boxes into the middle room and moved them back to the corner after we swept. "We'll go through these boxes later," I said. "I don't want to get too distracted from cleaning."

"Hey what ever happened to that picture of Grandpa?" I asked.

"Which one?" she said.

"The one with Grandpa and his family. You know, that big long one that was taken in Poland. It used to be tacked on to the attic wall. Right over there."

"Oh, that one. I haven't seen that picture in years. Somebody probably threw it away long ago."

"I was always amazed that it was taken in Poland and found it's way over here, I loved the way they're dressed, in military clothes and the women in babushkas. I'm fascinated by those old pictures, aren't you?"

"But you never cared much about old things."

"It didn't mean anything to me when I was a kid. But now it means much more. Didn't you ever try to look for it?"

"I guess I never thought much about it. It's been gone for years. What do you want it for? To show the boys what their ancestors looked like?"

"They don't care for old things. But some day they might. They're too busy with being teenagers right now. A friend of mine is really into genealogy. She was showing me some old, old photos of her grandparents and they were so neat. Then suddenly, that old photograph popped into my mind. I guess I thought it would still be there on the wall."

We were still sweeping and moving screens when I asked her, "Why didn't you tell us more about Grandpa? I didn't even know that was him in the picture so many years ago."

"You never asked and you didn't seem to care. When you were little, well, you wouldn't have understood. And then, in your teen years, you were always running off somewhere. Of course it was him. Who'd you think it was?"

"I never knew. I thought the people in the picture were just some strangers. Ray and I laughed at it when we were kids. He used it as a target to shoot BBs at. What were they doing in the picture?"

"I'm not sure. It was taken in Poland shortly before they made the trip to America. Grandpa and some of

My brother Ray and I playing in a washtub 1951.

his brothers were dressed in military uniforms. He was a horseman in the Polish Cavalry."

"I remember the women in the picture were dressed in peasant-style clothing with kerchiefs on their heads and stone faces that would scare anyone. Why did they leave? No one had ever told me. Did they ever talk about Poland?"

"Not much, they were too busy trying to make a living and trying to learn English. But Grandma did write to her sister Elizabeth. I remember how she would take paper and pen and wrap them neatly in a handkerchief. Then off she would go to visit a lady friend who would write a letter for her and mail it."

"She had a sister in Poland? I didn't know that. Did her sister write back? Did she have to have her friend read the letters?"

"No she could read. I wrote letters to my aunt after Grandma died. And she wrote back."

"Do you have the letters?"

"They're here somewhere."

I had to be careful of my footing. I tiptoed across the middle room. There were old boards not securely nailed down throughout the attic floor. One in particular kept tripping me in the center of the attic. When I stepped on one end the other flew up and made a quivering sound. My mother would laugh every time. "Watch out for that ...." she tried to warn me but it was always too late.

"That darn Conti!" I said. "Did Conti put in this floor? He should have done a better job pounding nails. What was the story on him anyway?"

"When I was born...you know the story. They already had me married off to Conti. I was promised to a man who was eighteen years older than I was."

"Why did they want you to marry him?"

"It was an old Polish custom. He was one of their boarders and he helped Grandpa build this house. I'm not sure if we owed him money or what. He later owned a shoe store. If I had married him, we would have been rich. Well, at least you kids would have had shoes."

"You mean I would have been Conti's daughter? Why didn't you marry him?"

"Because he was an old man, that's why."

We put the old wooden screens and iron bed frames against the chimney wall. I was tired, we had been carrying boxes and sorting things into piles for hours.

"Look at this, " she said. She began to pull out

dresses that were hanging on a wooden pole that ran from one end of the attic to a center post. Some were woolen; some were silk, and velvet. Taking each dress in turn, she held it up to her body and gave an account of the person that wore it. "Here, try this coat on," she said.

"Mom, I'm tired. I've been dragging boxes back

Mom's Wedding 1926.

and forth all day. Who's was it anyway?" It was black, shiny, and sleek. The fur was flat and coarse. "Is it mink?"

"No, it's sealskin. It was Auntie Ann's."

"Oh, my God. It smells like mothballs. Who did she think she was wearing a fancy sealskin coat?" By now I was modeling it for her. I pretended to be a high society chick from the thirties. "Like she was the queen of France or something."

"Lots of people had them. Here, these were hers too." She handed me a purse and an old hat, decorated with a large rhinestone and black netting across the top.

"Did they really wear these things? Where'd she get her money?"

"Of course, she had all the latest clothes. She was single and working near Downtown Minneapolis at the Cremette Company. She always wore hats."

I put the hat on and was carrying the purse. "Don't I look like Greta Garbo?" I said. We both had a good laugh.

I continued to look for Grandpa's picture whenever I could. My mother laughed at some of the odd places I looked in. She said, " It couldn't possibly fit in a crack that small." To divert me she said, "Maybe you'd like that old trunk over there, instead. You don't really need the picture. It's probably full of BB holes."

"I couldn't take that."

"I suppose the trunk is too old and junky to put in your house."

"It's not that I don't want it. But what would I do with a trunk? It's a part of this house. I just couldn't take it." I grabbed a rag and wiped away some of the dust from the trunk. Metal pieces were set in across the front with carved wood bands across the top and worn leather handles on the sides. The sheets of metal had a design that glittered like snowflakes. "It looks like someone made it."

"It is handmade. Your Grandpa built it. It came across the ocean in 1904. The year I was born. It was made in Poland."

"You mean it actually traveled all the way from Poland?"

"It certainly did, I thought you knew that?"

"Let's open it."

As I propped open the hinged lid, the worn leather handles almost disintegrated in my hand. The aroma of cedar mixed with a musty smell wafted up and filled my nostrils. She bent down a bit and lifted out a small compartment made of wood and covered in yellow flowered wallpaper. "Your Grandma used to keep a rosary and the family Bible in that special compartment," she said. "I found the rosary in there many years after she died."

"I wish I could have known them. Or at least knew more about them. I would have loved to experience the love that grandparents have for a grandchild."

"You are Them. You have your Grandpa's red hair and his gentle nature. And you like to tell stories and write things down the way your Grandma did."

"I guess that's true. You look tired Mom," I said. "Why don't you go downstairs? I can handle the rest."

"But how will you know what to do with it all?" Mom reached up to knock down a cobweb. "I guess I am getting tired," she said.

This was where it got harder. Every box had to be sorted through. I plopped down on the floor and began to sort. Here were the echoes of my mother's life and the several generations that lived here. She had saved everything—a proverb, a recipe for golapke, a picture of the mountains and a map of Poland during World War Two. I pulled out a small booklet of poems and began to turn the pages. The edges of each page were stained yellow. Between them a few flowers were pressed, and leaves whose green had faded leaving only the brittle veined skeleton. Was it a dried corsage from my sister's wedding or a lone flower from the graduation bouquets? Wrapped securely in an envelope was a lock of her mother's hair and the last letter she got from her brother, before he was killed in World War Two. I wondered how many tears had fallen on the bundles of cards and letters tied with faded ribbons and worn rubber bands.

When I got up my whole body was stiff and I still didn't want to stop looking. But it was starting to get late and there was only one bare light bulb hanging in the center of the attic. Then I heard Mom coming up the stairs. "It's way past time for lunch," she said as she handed me a metal tray with sandwiches.

"I don't want to stop and eat," I said. "What do you think of all the work I've done, doesn't it look great? I just have to do a little sweeping and move those boxes."

"I made pumpernickel toast and peanutbutter, and a bowl full of canned peaches. You always loved this when you were a kid."

"Well, okay as long as you've already made them. Boy I haven't had pumpernickel and peanutbutter since.... Well, probably since I left here. Where does the time go?"

"If you don't want that trunk I think I'm going to throw it away."

"You don't mean that. You can't throw it away." I

My Mom as a bridesmaid 1922.

RECIPE

Golabki (Cabbage Rolls)

1 Head Cabbage
1 1/4 lbs. Ground beef
1 cup cooked rice
1 Egg
1/4 cup onion
Salt and pepper

Cook cabbage in boiling salted water a few minutes to soften; drain. Place filling (beef, rice, egg, onion and seasonings) on each leaf and roll by folding sides. Secure with toothpicks or string. Place Golabki in greased roaster or dutch oven. Pour a little water and 1 can tomatoes or 1 can of tomato soup over them. Cover and bake in 350 degree oven for 1 1/2 to 2 hours.

My Uncle Eddy 1945.

was nowhere to be found. My mother looked at me and laughed as she pointed out the black dust that lined the edge of my nose.

"You know that trunk you wanted me to have, maybe I will take it home with me. We'll call it a payment for cleaning the attic. How old is it again?"

"It's the same age as I am, "she said. "79 years old. I'm sorry, we didn't find the picture."

"It's not a big deal, I'm taking the trunk," I said beaming.

I drove to my house happily with my prize possession. When I reached home I asked my son to help me bring it in from the car. As we slowly lifted it from of the trunk of the car, one of the handles broke off. Not realizing what it was or where it came from he asked, "What are you going to do with this piece of junk, Mom?"

I just smiled and thought to myself, when I was your age I wouldn't have appreciated it either. But I said to him, "Some day when you're older you will think of it as a treasure and a link to your heritage, the way I do. Your grandma says it's a piece of Poland."

My Mom and Auntie Anne dressed up for church 1956.

ate my peanutbutter toast that tasted pretty good and then stood up and went back to work.

When the end of the day came the attic was cleaner than I had ever seen it before. The boxes of cards and letters were neatly tucked away and the dust on the floor was swept clean. I knew my search had ended. I had looked in every nook and cranny but the picture

[1]Note- It was hard to forget that day, one of the last times we spent the entire day together. It was the summer before my mother died that I helped her clean the attic.

Quonset huts on 1500 Buchanan Street NE in 1946.

2 From Mansions to Quonset Huts: Northeast Minneapolis Houses

Northeast Homes Have Distinct Differences

Northeast Minneapolis housing is distinctly different from that in other parts of the city. The upper-middle class and business owners built the older houses in much of Minneapolis. But in old St. Anthony, now Northeast Minneapolis, many of the oldest houses were built for the working class.[2]

Some of those early homes have outstanding features, and the buildings represent a part of the city's heritage.

Many of the homes have social and architectural importance. Some are associated with people of past history. Even the influence of ethnicity is evident in the houses. Churches are the landmarks that mark the migration from Eastern Europe to Northeast Minneapolis. Each one has a unique style of architecture according to the influence of the groups of people who formed and built the church. Just because Northeast has a large number of working-class and middle-class homes doesn't mean that there are not many outstanding buildings that deserve to be preserved. Homes don't have to be elaborate mansions to be considered important. History surrounds us.

Carefully manicured lawns, vegetable gardens, and wildflowers are common in the area. Houses were functional, and the owners often added on a room here and there to keep pace with their growing families. Some of these houses have traveled from various parts of the city as turn-of-the-century residents moved houses (including one from the site on which the Guthrie Theater on Lowry Hill in South Minneapolis now sits) to Northeast Minneapolis, to pack more homes into this working-class neighborhood so convenient to the jobs offered by the breweries, railroads, and sawmills. Residents have worked hard to uncover the history of their homes and the neighborhood.

[2]Some of this section is taken from Patty Dean, "It is Here We Live," *Minnesota History,* Spring 2001 (57:244); *The Historic Garden District Gazette,* May 1993; Mike Anderson, "Neighbors Must Put Price on Northeast History," *Northeaster,* March 23, 1998.

Development of Central Avenue and "The Hill"

Streetcars Promote Development

A streetcar smashed into the front of a grocery store on 33rd and Johnson Street in the 1940s.

Railroad tracks in back of Broadway and Central Avenue Bridge in 1999.

There were so many railroad tracks in Northeast that it seemed unlikely that they would ever have residential developments. But in 1892, the Minneapolis City Council authorized the construction of a bridge at Broadway and Central that would go over the tracks in that area. It was the first of many bridges over dangerous grade crossings that had brought wagons, horses, pedestrians, and railroad traffic together.

Settlement beyond the early boundaries was encouraged when in the 1880s the streetcar service extended up Central Avenue as far as Twenty-sixth Avenue Northeast. Then in 1893, it extended to Fortieth Avenue Northeast into Columbia Heights. Central and Johnson were connected by streetcar in 1911 along Eighteenth Avenue Northeast to Twenty-eighth and Johnson.

Central Avenue then changed from having a few early frame stores into a principal artery lined with shops, stores, banks, and professional offices. There were also two Masonic buildings anchoring the prominent Lowry and Central intersection.

"New Boston"

One of the most prominent settlements in Northeast Minneapolis was "New Boston," because many people who came from Boston settled in this area. It was advertised as the "Garden Spot of Minneapolis," and was promoted by real estate dealers. There were only a handful of houses edging up the hill on about Eighteenth and Polk and Taylor Streets in the early 1800s. The New Boston Gazette defined the boundaries of the development as Eighteenth Avenue on the south, Fifth Street on the west, and the city limits on the north and east. Pontius Deming, park commissioner and president of the Minneapolis Park Board, described the district as having larger ornate homes on the hill and modest ones with green blinds scattered on the plains below. Nearly all of them had two lots enclosed by a wooden railing and a style of chimney that was known as the "Boston Top."

The first attempt of developing New Boston was in 1859 when "Hoyt's Addition" was platted. Harrison Street was laid out along a wagon trail and used by the father of A.W. Jesperson as a means of getting to and from a farm in Ham Lake. More was added to the development when in 1882 the "Blake Houses" were built. They were started by L. F. Menage, but were completed by John D. Blake. About 125 "Blake Houses" were scattered along Harrison Street, which later became Union Street and eventually Central Avenue. One of the early settlers painted the name, New Boston Dairy across his milk wagon, which was a common sight on the streets of New Boston.

One deterrent of early development in New Boston was a large peat bog that extended from Twenty-fourth and Fillmore to East Broadway. The bog spread several blocks in width and was prone to fire. In the summer, all traffic was detoured around the head of the bog on the stretch between Fillmore and Central along Twenty-fourth Avenue because of fires. In the winter, cars crossed the ice.

Several small commercial districts west of Central were developed by 1900. A grocery, butcher shop, barber, hardware store, restaurant, and bakery made up these storefronts. A meeting hall and professional services were also located in the centers. The primary neighborhood commercial centers at the turn of the century were Thirteenth Avenue and Second Street, Summer and Monroe Streets, Lowry and Second Street, and Broadway and Adams. The other developments evolved after the turn of the century at Twenty-second and Twenty-ninth and Johnson Streets. These one- and two-story buildings were a mixture of frame and brick structures with boomtown facades.

Johnson Street

The extension of the streetcar service around 1911 provided incentives for even more development. At the beginning of Johnson Street was a large industrial zone including a quarry at Fourteenth and Johnson, and from this point the elevation rose to its highest point of 977.3 feet at Thirty-fourth and Johnson. A full view of the city could be seen from the vicinity of Thirtieth and Fillmore, which was known as "The Hill." Large subdivisions were platted after the turn of the century, which attracted a large population of Scandinavians and Germans.

Johnson Street became the main artery that ran through the highest elevations of the Hill. In 1914, Dickenson and Gillespie offered building lots in the area for $100 to $325 with easy terms of one dollar per week. The construction of St. Anthony Boulevard improved the area even more. The lots were advertised as having high elevation and beautiful trees, close to streetcar lines with good schools and churches, within walking distance of the Soo Line shops, and boasting a boulevard that would eventually encircle the city.

The area of Twenty-ninth and Johnson Street remained a compact commercial area; it offered a bakery, grocery, hardware, drugstores, gasoline service stations, and other small businesses. The addition of Fire Station #27 in 1915 and the Hollywood Theater in 1935 added to its importance, and many churches were located within few blocks of the intersection.

Boardinghouses

Many industries employed unmarried and transient workers, who often lived in Northeast boardinghouses. Thirteen were listed in the 1895 Minneapolis City Directory. Most were operated by women and dispersed along Central Avenue. Boarders ate their meals at a common table, chatted or read newspapers in the same parlor, and stood in line to share bathrooms. Books, magazines, songs, and jokes frequently lampooned the table manners of boarders who ate in self-defense, competing for a better share of the food. The practice of reaching across a neighbor's plate to snare a muffin or a potato was known throughout the land as "the boardinghouse reach."

Junction Boarding House on 26th Central Avenue. Maggie Wheeler, Hired girl, Adeline Wheeler, Marjorie Wheeler, Frank Unruh, Addie Wheeler Unruh, William Unruh 1907.

Corner of Lowry and Central Avenue with trolley tracks 1935.

Double Bungalows

Builder Robert H. McGuffie introduced a bungalow duplex or the double bungalow to Northeast Minneapolis in 1928 at 2625-27 Johnson Street. It was described as having "English Architecture," with a stucco, brick, and stone exterior. It was the first of many constructed by McGuffie and others. A great number of duplexes were built in Northeast to house extended family members who wanted to live together.

Pre-Fab Housing

The housing shortage of post World War II was reflected in Northeast Minneapolis emergency housing projects. Temporary housing was provided, including a 1947 prefab project near the Soo Line tracks on Thirty-seventh Avenue on Polk, Taylor, and Johnson streets Northeast. The project housed 166 families with 310 adults and 653 children. The houses, which rented for $42 to $48 per month, were classified as semi-permanent.

Arts and Crafts Houses

The Arts and Crafts movement was a philosophy that began in Britain but soon found its way to the United States, according to Patty Dean in her article, "It is Here We Live." Between 1875 and 1920, the movement found a hospitable home in the Upper Midwest. This type of home was fundamental to the Arts and Crafts movement, which emphasized the beauty of "handmade architectural ornament" that reflected human labor. Arts and Crafts reformers believed that "societal ills could be remedied by improved home environments," which began with creating and arranging household articles that were useful, beautiful, and simple.

The Upper Midwest was viewed as a "garden of the world," where nature, independence, and confidence intertwined to produce "the good life" for the growing urban middle class. Prosperity was considered the result of the richness of the land and the industry of the people.

Arts and Crafts houses showed that beauty could be attained without spending a lot of money. The 1899 issue of Keith's magazine and The Craftsman sold standard plans for building bungalows so that individuals without architects could build their own Arts and Crafts home. Hallmarks of these homes were fireplaces, open floor plans, built-in cabinets, bookshelves, and closets to maximize space. They also featured clean lines and natural beauty.

Central Avenue

Central Avenue reached its peak in the mid-1950s. But after World War II as cars became more plentiful and cheaper, more people could afford to buy cars and travel greater distances. Competition from suburban shopping centers like St. Anthony Village and Apache Plaza began to diminish the avenue's customer base.

Fidelity State Bank at Twenty-fourth and Central was established in 1917 and Central State Bank at Twenty-fourth and Central was organized in 1928. In the 1920s and 1930s, Central Avenue became a popular location for car dealerships. Automobile repair and gasoline stations were established on nearly every block. In the 1940s and 1950s there were 13 gas stations on Central Avenue.

The Arion Theater at 2417 Central Avenue was a popular destination. Grocery, jewelry, clothing stores, and other retail businesses were established. The YMCA opened a branch in 1919 at 2334 Central Avenue.

The Central Avenue branch Library, provided by Carnegie money, opened at 22nd and Central in November of 1915. It replaced the New Boston branch, which was a rented quarters since 1907. In the early 1970s it was replaced by the new Northeast Community Library, a one-story building designed to fit the craftsman like tone of Northeast.

Accident scene at the intersection of 34th and Tyler Street NE in 1936.

Pre-fab housing on Fillmore Street NE, 1948.

Old Foster House, once the second oldest house on East-side of Minneapolis 427 Main Street NE. Grandma Catherine Erb is sitting on porch, 1880s.

*Melrose Flats13-23 Fifth Street NE built by Charles Sedg-
wick in 1890. Photo taken 1999*

*Beaux Arts Fourplex 400-402 Eighth Avenue NE
built in 1910. Photo taken 2001*

*Flemish Duplex on 415 Eighth Avenue NE
built in 1910. Photo taken 2001*

*P. W. Lein Italianate Duplex on 444-46 Madison Street NE,
built in 1888. Photo taken 1974*

Queen Anne Architecture

Victorian homes in the Queen Anne style were built in Minnesota from about 1880 to 1910. Bigger and fancier than most styles of homes, they were built on large lots away from downtown. They are known for their windows of all shapes and sizes, large number of rooms, high ceilings, towers, porches, balconies, and decorative trim. They also usually have irregular shapes, two or more stories, and a complex roof of peaks, gables, turrets, and "fish scale" shingles. Often, a different siding covers each story. A common Victorian feature from New England coastal towns but sometimes used in the Midwest was a widow's walk, which is a small deck or platform with a rail around it, built onto the roof and reached through a trap door and ladder in the attic. Widow's walks were especially common along the coastal areas and used to observe ships, but were given that name because that's where the wives of fishermen stood to watch for their husbands to return from the sea.

Queen Anne houses with prominent corbelled chimneys were found along Taylor and Fillmore Streets and modest white homes lined Polk and other cross streets between Eighteenth and Twenty-seventh Avenues. A corbel is a projection made of wood or stone that is common in mosques and other types of buildings. These corbels are arranged as a series of intersecting miniature arches. The houses in the Lincoln Street supplement and south of Twenty-fifth Avenue were built by J. D. Blake. They sold for $600 down and $26 per month for eight years.

Queen Anne houses were built in Logan Park and on Main and Marshall in the 1890s. High-styled examples of Queen Anne, Colonial Revival, and Shingle Style houses were built on Lowry and Central and east of Polk Street. This was the heart of New Boston and typically housed Central Avenue businessmen, as well as many artisans and trades people.

Queen Anne house on 1228 Adams Street NE, built in 1885 Note* Eyebrow windows Photo taken in 2001.

Arts and Crafts homes on the east side of 26th and Arthur Street NE, 1939.

*BF Nelson Memorial Settlement House
518 Marshall Street NE, 1937.*

*The Castle" at 1501-18th Avenue NE was restored in
1986. The Queen Anne Victorian was built in 1889 by
John Cook. The brick exterior is rare; most Queen Anne's
are made of wood.*

A Few Noteworthy Homes

HARRIET MOUSSEAU HOME
915 Second Street Northeast

Once the oldest house in Minneapolis, the Harriet Mousseau house was built by Alexander Cloutier, a French-Canadian settler. Harriet Mousseau was born in the house in 1841 and occupied it until her death in 1937 at the age of 96. Although some have alleged that Harriet was the first white child born in Minneapolis, that "first" has been credited to Harriet Godfrey. This house was the first one started in Minneapolis, but a shortage of lumber delayed construction, and the Godfrey House ended up being completed first. The Godfrey House stands as a Pioneers Museum in Chute Square located at University and Central Avenue.

Harriet's daughter, Frances (Fanny) Mousseau LaFlair, used to talk of sitting on the porch and watching the steamboats come up the river. There was nothing between her house and the river. The Red River Ox Cart Trail, which fur traders traveled regularly from Pembina, North Dakota to St. Paul and St. Anthony in the early 1850s, later became Marshall Street.

Alongside the house ran the Great Northern Railroad main line. The old Mousseau house was torn down in 1963, and the land and adjoining property was used for construction of a two-and-a-half story apartment building of 35 units built by Kenneth Nordling.

LEBLANC HOUSE
302 University Avenue Northeast

LeBlanc House 302 University Avenue NE.

French-Canadian builder William LeBlanc, an engineer with the river lumber mills, built this Queen Anne-Dutch Colonial home in 1896. LeBlanc is best known for his involvement in the reconstruction of historic Our Lady of Lourdes Church, built originally as a Universalist church and the oldest church in continuous use in Minneapolis.

The LeBlanc House was one of the first ones built in the area after a fire on nearby Boom Island and Northeast Minneapolis in 1893. It narrowly escaped the fate of many homes in the 1960s when the ill-fated freeway plan to link I-35W and I-94 resulted in the destruction of hundreds of homes. The "Lennon Sisters"–no relation to the well-known singers-lived there for 50 years, until 1979.

Barb Zahasky and Bob Shulstad bought the LeBlanc House in 1990, restored the Victorian home, and turned it into a bed and breakfast. The house contains the original woodwork, seven stained glass windows, the original archways into three second-floor bedrooms, and the original hardwood floors. Zahasky, who was interested in the Victorian period, spent many evenings at the Minneapolis Public Library looking at books on that period, and then began adding to her collection of furniture. A flyer from the bed and breakfast says: "Antique furniture from the 1850s and 1860s makes the house look like it may well have looked for its original owners."

Inside the LeBlanc House are two connecting parlors graced with Victorian antiques, including rosewood and inlaid chairs, a pump organ, and an old Victrola with push-button record selector. It has three bedrooms with carved walnut beds and lace-curtained windows. A 10-foot fireplace mantel and a large amount of period needlework are displayed throughout the house. In summer, the yard outside the house explodes with blooming boulevard color and award-winning gardens.

The LeBlanc House, now owned by Marsha and Peter Carlson, provides a fitting welcome to a 200-square block area of Minneapolis that has become known as the "Garden District of Northeast." The boundaries for this district are from Third Avenue to Twenty-third Avenue and the Mississippi River to Monroe Street. Within the Garden District is the "Historic Garden District." This area, from Broadway to Seventeenth and Washington to Monroe, contains one of the finest collections of late Victorian homes in the city. This unique district consists of homeowners, businesses, church groups, and gardeners, whose motto is "Keep Northeast Beautiful!" Some feature ethnic gardens.

The house has been featured in Midwest Living, Victorian Homes, and Mpls St. Paul magazines. The LeBlanc House has visitors from all over the world.

"MUENSE'S CASTLE"
656 Jefferson Northeast

Muense Castle 656 Jefferson Street NE, 1999.

What is now known as "Muense's Castle" on Jefferson was built in 1880. Although missing the traditional moat and drawbridge, the home features curious and colorful decorations, which make this home one of the most unusual on the East side. Werner and Thekla Muense moved into the house in 1956. Muense, a German-born craftsman who came to the United States in 1953, started enhancing his house in 1967.

Werner had become interested in carving when he was a boy growing up in Pommern, Germany, located on the north coast. In his "castle," he worked almost every day on his favorite hobby, reconditioning old figurines and creating new ones. A black-and-white fence surrounds fanciful and playful elements that look as though they came straight out of a storybook. A miniature cannon and a Civil War soldier guard the American flag, and nearby, a wooden deer gracefully jumps a short white fence. A water wheel at the entrance turns by power generated with rain runoff from the roof, while miniature figures from a cave village watch. On one side stands a flower-covered wishing well with a totem pole proudly mounted on the front. On the garage roof, a small thatched hut has lighted windows to illuminate the nighttime activity of a miniature family. A five-foot-long cannon perched on the balcony of the house guards the front gate.

The Muense home interior is also unique. It is decorated with tapestries, flags, and a lifelike stuffed fox and pheasant. Werner Muense died in 1999.

Close up of Muense figurines, 2001.

MCMILLAN-LACY-BROS MANSION
677 Thirteenth Avenue

McMillan-Lacy-Bros Mansion 677-13th Avenue NE, 1999.

Early settlers and businessmen Richard and Samuel Chute acquired a vast tract of land in the nineteenth century, stretching from modern Washington to Quincy streets and from Broadway to Twenty-second Avenue Northeast. They hoped that city expansion would make it valuable some day. In 1884, they sold the land to a group of investors which included Putnam D. McMillan (father of the Putnam D. McMillan, who helped found General Mills) on the condition that he build a house that would anchor an elite neighborhood to rival Portland Avenue in Minneapolis and Summit Avenue in St. Paul.

Builder C. W. Lunquist started building the mansion in 1886. Modest homes at that time were under $1,000; the mansion cost $4,500. Another $300 went toward indoor plumbing, which cost as much as some entire houses. The mansion stood by itself at that time, surrounded by prairie.

The interior is done in the Eastlake style with clean and natural lines and nature motifs that contrasted with the heavy ornamentation of earlier Victorian homes. John Bradstreet, Minneapolis's premier designer, designed the original four rooms. The first owner was the Phineas B. Lacy family. Lacy was a prominent lumberman who bought the house in 1887. Lacy and his partner owned a sash and door company and Pineville Lumber Company. The Depression of the mid-1890s put an end to its profitable years, and Lacy lost the house in a tax sale that year.

The second owner was the William Bros family. Bros owned a boiler works located on Nicollet Island. The family immediately updated the electricity and plumbing. In 1916, they asked Lunquist to build an addition. The second and third floors were added. Although the original globes of the lamp were lost, they were almost identical to the ones in the Glensheen Mansion in Duluth. It also contained a beam ceiling and mural of a rustic mountain scene. The family used the third floor as a ballroom, and stories recall the grandness of the Bros parties. In 1924, the Bros family moved to south Minneapolis, where their friends lived.

The next owners used the mansion as the Hill-Young School, a Boardinghouse School to help children overcome speech defects. It closed in 1929. Fred and Ida Erickson then bought the house in 1931, and ran it as a boardinghouse until the mid-1940s. During its 60 years as a boardinghouse, at various times it had from seven to thirteen apartments.

Many neighbors assumed that Thomas Lowry lived in the mansion at one time, but there is no evidence that he had any connection to the house. The confusion may have come about because a nearby stable housed the horses that pulled streetcars (and Lowry, of course, was the man most responsible for the city's streetcar system); and a designer with a similar name was connected to the house, so people assumed he was the more famous Lowry.

The next owners, Joe Brodsky and Al Kremer, restored the mansion in 1994. It took eight weeks of working round the clock to restore it to the grandeur that its builders originally intended. Special features of the house include unusual carved woodwork throughout, a magnificent staircase, decorative stained-glass windows, and six bedrooms and six bathrooms.

QUONSET HUTS

The housing shortage following World War II forced many families into military-style Quonset huts. They were ugly but necessary. Millions of servicemen were returning home from the war in 1945-46, and the housing industry couldn't keep up with the demand. One hundred and forty-six Quonset huts were erected at Sixteenth and Buchanan Street Northeast in 1946. The walls and roofs were heavily corrugated metal. Most were found on college campuses, but some were located in a residential neighborhood from Fifteenth to Seventeenth and Buchanan, to Lincoln and Johnson Street, which is now an athletic field. Priority was given to veterans according to their needs. Each hut was divided into two apartments with an entrance at each end. Each unit contained two bedrooms, a bath, and a combined kitchen-living room. It rented for about $50 monthly with utilities furnished.

Kitchen inside Quonset hut in 1950.

People wondered what effect Quonset huts would have on the lives of the families forced to live in such tight, drab quarters. But veterans attending the University of Minnesota and their families desperately needed a place to live while they were going to school. In the fall of 1945, University Villages sprang up in all parts of the city, and those who lived there were proud of their makeshift homes. Some even painted their living room walls bright yellow, which helped them forget that they curved inward and their windows were at an alarming angle to the floor. Barracks veterans claimed that color made all the difference between a

Bedroom inside Quonset hut in 1951, complete with Bunk Twin beds, Baseball radio, and rag doll. One of the first four families moved into the complex on Christmas Eve 1946. Hatch way panels 6 feet high and 22 inches wide were cut directly into existing wall.

dismal existence and a place they were proud of. Slip-covering their hand-me-down furniture in bright prints helped, too.

Veteran families lived on $105 a month GI allowance for married students, or the $120 granted

veterans with children. Many worked to add extra income. Orange crates disguised as desks with linoleum tops, full-skirted dressing tables, bookshelves, and children's toy boxes cropped up in almost every room. A bookcase made of boards and bricks cost very little.

Living Room inside Quonset hut in 1950.

Curtains and draperies for these windows required some calculating. Residents experimented with furniture and color in ways they never would have thought of if everyone else weren't doing it. But they all waited optimistically for the chance to put these ideas into practice in a plain, ordinary house.

The Baby Boom and the economy both grew, and there was a mass exodus to the suburbs. Most homebuyers were dream rich and money poor. The Federal Housing Authority (FHA) required a 20 percent down payment in 1934. In the 1950s, it was lowered to 3 percent. And the Veterans Administration Program in 1954 offered the ultimate, the no-down-payment loan.

Grace Manor, 1507 Lowry Avenue Northeast. Mrs. Emily Holmquist organized the Women's Relief Society in 1906. They purchased a house on the crest of the hill near Lowry and Johnson Street and turned it into the Scandinavian Relief Home. The exterior was replaced with red brick and a white portico porch was added. in 1961, the name was changed to the Union Home For The Aged and more recently to Grace Manor. Photo taken in 2002

2204 Marshall Street NE, built in 1900.

The "Painted Lady" Victorian built in 1890s
1226 Adams Street NE, photo taken in 2002.

2601 Ulysses Street NE, built in 1913.

Dusenka Bar fire 1828 Fourth Street NE on February 10, 1944.

3 Connections-The Places We Remember

Connections has continued to be a favorite section of all three books: Heart and Hard Work: Memories of Nordeast Minneapolis, Pride and Tradition: More Memories of Northeast Minneapolis, and Roots and Ties: A Scrapbook of Northeast memories. It was created from the initial comments that people made about the places they felt connected to. Some of the buildings are still standing and others have been torn down. But to the people of Northeast they are etched in their memory.

Saloons and Cafes

ARTHUR'S FOUR SEASONS, NOW GASTHOF ZUR GEMUTLICHKEIT
2300 University Avenue Northeast

Known for having the longest bar in the Twin Cities and as the "Home of the Onion Ring," Arthur's was one of the biggest and best restaurants in town. Within a six-block radius of Arthur's, were Jax, Little Jack's, the Edgewater, and the Wig and Bottle.

Mr. Godlewski was the original owner of the restaurant, which began in 1912. He later owned Grumpy's at 2200 Northeast Fourth Street. In 1939, Joe Worwa bought the place and called it Joe's Corner Bar. A large neon sign that read "Cocktails," and an attractive front concealed the fact that this restaurant was a stucco bungalow, just like the other buildings surrounding it in the neighborhood. It was well known for its lively atmosphere and good service. On each table stood a red lamp, and when they were all lit, they illuminated the room to provide a

One of the longest bars in the Twin Cities in 1978.

43

soft, intimate dining experience. Prices were not high, so it became a popular place to go on Saturday nights. It then became well known as the "Home of Dinner Steaks." Worwa's Skylight Room and Cedar Room were available for party groups.

During the 1960s, you could take the bus to University of Minnesota Gopher games from Worwa's, and a special menu would be served for home football games. In 1952, the middle portion of the building was added, and in 1961, the north portion.

Three brothers ran Arthur's Four Seasons, Gordy, Doug and Tom Solz, 1978.

In 1968, it became Arthur's. Three brothers, Gordy, Doug, and Tom Solz bought it and named it after their dad, Arthur Solz, so they would be on the first page of the Yellow Pages. With two dining rooms and a paneled lounge with leather-upholstered furniture, they could accommodate 250 people even without the banquet rooms.

Fifty-three items were listed on the menu, including Polish onion soup. The onion rings were 95 cents and included a declaration that they were "a dozen of the best in the world." The preparation of the onion ring became a ritual. The technicians in charge were both named Annie. These two neighborhood women came in each day to prepare the rings for frying. To keep the identification straight, the staff nicknamed them German Annie and Polish Annie. Their status as queens of the kitchen became firmly established when one of the younger cooks tossed a hot french-fried potato in their direction. Onion-ring production promptly came to a halt and an uproar ensued. Peace was not restored until management issued strict orders not to mess with the onion department. Other crises came up when grown men who regularly came in for lunch would actually fight over who would get the rice rolls in the basket of assorted rolls.

Gasthof zur Gemutlichkeit

Mario Pierchalski turned the place into Gasthof zur Gemuetlichkeit in 1992. He was born in Poland and had worked as a cook in Germany. Gasthof has multigenerational music, rowdy crowds, and rich Deutschland decor. In Bavarian dialect, the restaurant name, roughly translated, means "a guesthouse with warm feeling, where you drink and laugh with your friends." It serves imported beer and German food such as Schlemmerplatter, Wiener schnitzel, sauerbraten, excellent red cabbage, and apple strudel. The strolling accordionist plays rambunctious songs for the crowd.

Mario's Keller Bar, a party room downstairs, features polka bands on the weekends and modern rock midweek. Some of the local bands that have been successful are Groove Union, Big Wu, Tubby Esquire Trio, and Geyser featuring Justin Allen, Nate Allenson Jordy Anderson, and Andy Kieley (the author's son).

Local Northeast Band-Geyser, in 2002.

B & B BAR AND CAFÉ
1528 University Avenue Northeast

Two guys from a neighboring business came in for a cold one at the B and B, 1940s.

The B & B originally started at what is now known as The River Gardens on Marshall Street. It was in the mid 1940s that it was moved to 15th and University. Julian Boyda and Danny Bucknack originally owned the bar and it wasn't until the early 1950s that Julian bought out Danny and became the sole owner. Julian's brother Frank helped out at the bar for many years.

When Julian's daughters, Janice Carroll, Nancy Nelson and Elaine Stano were in 7th and 8th grade, their job was to go down in the basement of the bar and peel garbage pails full of potatoes. The pails were used only for potatoes and stored in the big walk in a cooler that was located down there. When they finished peeling three garbage pails (30 gallon size) they were white from their heads to their knees from all the starch that came from the potatoes.

They didn't mind doing the job too much, only when their parents forgot that they were down there peeling and shut off the lights. Then when they screamed Julian and Caroline would remember and turn the lights back on. Oh what a relief!

Julian Boyda would cut all of his meat that he used at the restaurant. The packing company would come

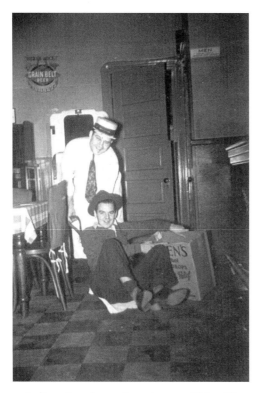

Owner Julian Boyda and customer Obie, Clowning around at the B and B in the 1940s

to the back door with a side of beef or pork and put them on the table in the kitchen and Julian would start carving. His dad owned Boyda's Meat on Marshall Street so that is why he knew how to cut that big side of beef. It wasn't until he was about to sell the bar that

he finally had to give into modern times. It just didn't feel right to him to have his meat brought in pre-cut and in just the right size and shape. He liked to do his own cutting.

He was famous for his home made soups, barbecued ribs, pork tenderloins, and deep-fried chicken and shrimp. Till this day when his daughters think about his deep-fried chicken their mouths water. Their dad told them the recipe for it, but no matter

A group came in for refreshments, 1940s.

how hard they try, there's something that is just not right. Maybe it's because their dad is not making it.

Every now and then they meet some of the people that came into the bar and they get to talking and the people always mention how they miss Julian's home made ribs, or his shrimp or chicken.

Julian and Caroline Boyda sold it to Denny & Don in the late 1970s.

BERGMAN'S SWEDISH BAKERY
2652 Johnson Street Northeast

Ansine and Walter Bergman were born in Sweden in 1890, married in 1924, and soon after came to the United States and Minneapolis. When Walter lost his job in 1943, he and Ansine took over a vacant store

Ansine, Walter and son Lloyd Bergman and one of their employees in the 1930s.

from which they sold bakery goods. His brother, Alfred Bergman, had a bakery on Thirty-ninth and Lake Street in Minneapolis, and every day he delivered fresh bakery goods to them. Then one day, he said, "I can't deliver any more." Ansine and Walter were distraught and complained to their friend Gabriel Burman, Swedish-born plumber on Twenty-second and

Johnson Street. "Why don't you just start your own bakery?" he asked. Ansine Bergman started to cry. "We don't have any money." "I will loan you $1,000 and help you buy the equipment," he replied.

Lloyd Bergman delivering bread in the 1930s.

They knew nothing about baking–but soon learned. Ansine took cake decorating at Dunwoody Vocational School and became an accomplished baker. One of their employees was Vivian Graves, who had once owned a bakery but had to close it because of hard times. She taught them a great deal about baking. The bakery closed a year after Walter died in 1952 and the building was sold.

CHILI BOWL
Spring and Monroe Streets

In the late 1940s, Gladys Vollmer and Monica M. Kulig were "second mothers" for a crew of rowdy teenagers who came into their restaurant. It was a hangout for many of the fellows, whether they were going to school or just hanging around. There were rough parts of Minneapolis back then. A lot of the boys had been on probation or sent to Glen Lake Reform School for Boys. Gladys and Monica would often lend the boys their car so they wouldn't go out and steal one. They served free hamburgers to kids with no money, or lent them a buck to go to the movies. Most of the gang went straight, thanks in part to Vollmer and Kulig. The women encouraged the guys to be ambitious and one even became an alderman.

The group of boys who hung out at the Chili Bowl lost track of the two women when they moved away from Northeast Minneapolis because they never knew their last names. Then one of the guys found the Glad-Mars Cafe in Hamel and recognized the owners: Vollmer and Kulig.

Vollmer said, "They used to slice our tires and fill our locks with water when it was 20 below. Yet we loved those kids. They told us their troubles and their plans." On January 28, 1967, more than 70 members of "the gang" paid off an old debt by throwing a banquet for the two women at the Golden Key Club in Blaine. They never realized how many characters they helped mold.

CREST EAT SHOP
2311 Central Avenue Northeast

Crest Café looking southeast along Central Avenue toward the intersection of 23rd Avenue NE in 1952

This family operation was bought by Elsie Faye and Clarence Kopp in 1952. Elsie Faye also had the support of her four children and Alice Brown, who started working there one month after they opened the cafe. Alice was her right arm. Her oldest son, Clarence, worked on the grill until he opened the L Cafe in North Minneapolis. Her oldest daughter, Joyce Varhol, worked at the cafe full time, even with a family of six. Her son, James, and daughter, Sandra, worked at the cafe when they were needed also, even though they had other jobs.

Faye shifted her time around to fill in when necessary. But she enjoyed the early shift because it was a busy time and because the "Old Crow Corner" convened then–about eight old-timers who for years came in early. They got into discussions about the high cost of living, news in the paper, and a variety of other topics over their coffee. They were noisier than any group of teenagers. According to Faye, the Crest Cafe employees and customers were "just like one big family." After her husband's death in 1967, Faye closed the shop for two and a half weeks. Then she reopened, realizing that she didn't want the place to deteriorate after the two of them had worked side by side through the years to build it up. The Crest closed in 1972.

THE EDGEWATER INN AND THE EDGEWATER EIGHT
2420 Marshall Street Northeast

There was a time when the Edgewater Inn was a five-star restaurant and high on the smart crowd's list of appropriate choices for anniversaries, birthdays, and other festive occasions. When it opened in 1960, it was the only eating establishment located directly on the waterfront. Business didn't really pick up until Gilbert Swenberger and Al Sheehan decided to introduce a group that came to be known as the Edgewater Eight, a crew of energetic show business hopefuls who sang and danced their way into the hearts of Twin Citians. Gil was the former manager of Schiek's in downtown Minneapolis.

West Side Story Prompts Edgewater Beginnings

It all started in the fall of 1962 when Gary Schultz directed the Bloomington Civic Theater in West Side Story. Al Sheehan was in the audience during one of the performances. He loved the production so much

that he asked Gary Schultz and Fred Smith to put together an audition for the Edgewater Inn. Four of the original eight singers came from the Bloomington production of West Side Story. Many of them had been performing at a storefront theater on Nicollet Avenue and Lake Street.

Reviewers and the audience loved the first show, made up of Broadway hits. When Swenberger saw the audition, he signed a contract to use the Edgewater Eight in the Edgewater Inn. Each new show had its beginning when Sheehan and Schultz would pick a theme. It might be a musical comedy, such as Mame, or a show created around a season, a holiday, a period of time, or a country. They would decide what songs should be in the show.

They did music from Cabaret, Bye Bye Birdie, Sound of Music, and Hair. While most Edgewater shows ran for three weeks, many were held over because word-of-mouth publicity made them so popular.

Jean Mayer, who made the costumes, was fast, efficient, and creative. She had the responsibility of making two sets of costumes for each member for each show, plus any specialty costumes. The arranger was Red McLeod, and the Don McGrane Orchestra provided the music. Frank Oliveri was the piano player for many years, and he arranged the music when McLeod left. The original choreography was by Nancy Raddatz, who came from West Side Story.

On Both Sides of the Lights

The hallmark of the Edgewater shows was the use of stepladders and cubes of various sizes and colors for the stage settings, giving the stage a modern look, but the settings were conceived more out of necessity

The Edgewater Eight, Front-Kathy Watson, Robert Hanson, Jackie Posz, Back-Xenia Mirza, Dave Burleigh, Tom Netherton, Dominic Castino, Susan Schaeffer, 1960s.

than artistic inspiration. A thrust stage placed the performers almost into the audience, and it was raised so people could see them. The players themselves would rearrange the props between sets. When new performers came in, there were collisions. One night after a set change, a young woman who was supposed to sing a solo was instead flat on her back under a ladder.

It was always fun to see who would be sitting at the center table in the front row, since many well-known people went there. Some came to the restaurant "dressed to the nines" in diamonds and minks. There were those people who were going out just to be seen. Jim Marshall of the Minnesota Vikings and his gorgeous wife came often. But it was also a family show and people brought their kids. It was a polite audience, which dressed in ties and sport coats. Sometimes three generations, just coming from church, would parade in.

The Edgewater Eight became so popular it was hard to get reservations. For many of these young performers, it was their first job. It was a rigorous schedule, thirteen shows a week with two each night and three on Saturdays. The group included four women and four men who could sing and dance. The original Edgewater Eight were Kathy Watson Castino, Robert Hansen, Jackie Posz Hansen, Judy Frank, Jan Howe, Lynn Fitch, Jim Mariner, and Dave Crawford. Some of the performers over the years were Dominic Castino, Jackie Steele, Don Bakke, Joanie Knutson, and Frank Greczena. In recent years, the group has been performing at various places for reunions.

More than 1,000 different performers got their start with the Edgewater Eight. The original director, Gary Schulz, had a knack for picking good performers. Those who came in inexperienced and "rough" began to blossom after performing alongside so many talented people.

The restaurant served 250 people in the main dining room with a piano bar and cocktail lounge on the upper level and private dining rooms on the lower level. An ad from 1966 advertised show and dinner at the Edgewater for $3.49. It closed only when there was a snowstorm. A tornado hit the Edgewater in 1965. Strangely enough, 10 or 20 people showed up, so the Edgewater Eight entertained them until the storm worsened, and they took cover under the tables and finally had to quit when the roof blew off.

When business started to dwindle, the dinner theater was sold in 1980. The new restaurant was called Edgewater East and did not feature the Edgewater Eight. The restaurant changed hands a few times, became a Chinese restaurant, and was virtually forgotten by everyone but Northeasters. The building was boarded up in 1989 and torn down in 1994.

HAMBURGER JOINT
2519 Central Avenue Northeast

Tom Sullivan opened the Hamburger Joint in 1978. He wanted to turn it into more than just another place to go for a hamburger or a sandwich, so he asked area residents to donate old photographs, paintings, or other wall displays that depicted Northeast Minneapolis in the 1930s, especially pictures of old buildings along Central Avenue.

The building that the Hamburger Joint was located in was originally the Band Box restaurant, which was in a building whose history dates back nearly 100 years. Part of the old ceiling from the old Band Box restaurant was used in the new restaurant. The Band Box slogan was "three for a dime, anytime."

Sullivan was born and raised in Northeast and opened his first Hamburger Joint restaurant in 1976.

He owned three, including the one at the Central Avenue location. The other two were at 1120 Lowry Avenue North and at St. Clair and Snelling Avenues in St. Paul (now the St. Clair Broiler). Booths were custom made at Howard's Cabinet Shop in Northeast, and draped to add privacy for diners. Later Sullivan owned Central Avenue Liquors, Kroger's Appliances, and Sully's Pub.

JIMMY'S ON FOURTH
1828 Northeast Fourth Street,

Jimmy's on Fourth started out as Dusenka's Bar around the turn of the century and was one of the first to get a liquor license when Prohibition was lifted in 1933, according to former owner Jim Dusenka. His father, Frank Dusenka, Sr., rented the building from the Grain Belt Brewery in 1933. The Salvation Army rented the upstairs and a pool hall was downstairs.

The two sons, Jim and Frank, Jr., took over the bar in 1950 when their dad, Jimmy Dusenka, died. They bought the building in 1955 and remodeled it by cutting off the top of the building. They also installed a stone front and put leather-covered seats in the booths. Every year, they served sandwiches and put on a feast for the Russian New Year on January 7. Musician Eddy Marshall was popular and entertained the crowd with his concertina. He also played at Nye's.

In 1972, the Dusenka family sold the bar to Joe and Emily Worwa. In 1975, the Worwas sold it to Jimmy Harris, who once owned a flower shop on Central Avenue. Harris renamed it Jimmy's.

Jimmy's today is known for its "Little Polish Deli," and some of the specialties include kielbasa and large

Dusenka's Bar at 1828 NE Fourth Street in 1936. Frank Dusenka Sr., Frank Jr., and two bartenders.
Ties and aprons were mandatory for all who worked in the bar.

hot dogs with soup and sandwiches. Jimmy's serves a Vegas-style shrimp cocktail during the week and crab cocktail on weekends. On Christmas Eve, Jimmy provides a homemade sauerkraut hot dish, and during Easter season, a homemade horseradish. He donates beer every year for the Holy Cross Fall Festival.

For the last 25 years, he has sponsored many sports (men, women, and mixed) leagues-softball, baseball, bowling, broomball, and basketball. He recently received an award for his work in sponsoring the Peewee Baseball Classic for 25 years.

MY PLACE ON BROADWAY , NOW UNCLE FRANKIES FAMILY RESTAURANT
728 Broadway Street Northeast

My Place on Broadway in 1999.

My Place on Broadway was started in 1938 by Larry and Laurie Paul and Mike Kosticks, who owned the bar for many years. In the 1960s, Mike Sullivan owned it. A fire in 1997 destroyed so much of it that it took a year and a half to rebuild. Once a strictly "3-2 bar," it was upscaled and served microbrewery beers on tap.

Mike Abramovitz bought the place in April of 1999. He worked hard to build it up. He installed a new kitchen and fryers and also rebuilt the stairs and exterior of the building. It became a working-person's bar and family restaurant. My Place was known for its hamburgers, which were considered by some the best in town. They also served Chi-town hot dogs, chicken drummies, and delicious buffalo wings. My Place had a game room with video games, a jukebox, and a large-screen TV. In the fall there were Viking football specials with drawings at half-time. In January of 2002 Jay Grobstein and Ellen Meehan bought My Place and turned it into Uncle Frankies, a friendly family restaurant. Some of their specialties are Chicago hot dogs, beef and deli sandwiches, malts and phosphates. They also own Café Erte', a fine dining steakhouse on 13th and University Avenue.

Artist Community Blooms

ART-A-WHIRL

"The artists are coming Northeast" became a familiar saying in the mid-1990s, and the arts environment in Northeast began to change. Art-a-Whirl began in 1995 when David Felker, who opened one of the first art galleries in the Thorpe Building, came up with the idea of a Northeast gallery tour. People could visit artists at work in their own studios. The artists could also teach, demonstrate, talk about, and sell their work. Felker motivated others to join him in making this studio tour come alive. Walt Dziedzic, city council member from Northeast, was also instrumental in getting Art-a-Whirl started. When Felker met with him at city hall, Dziedzic was impressed with the idea and helped raise money for the first year.

What started out as 20 buildings in the beginning has grown to 300 artists in 95 buildings in the year 2001. It is a great social network with food, fun, and even music provided. It is held every year in May, and people come from all over the Twin Cities to visit the store fronts, private homes, year-round art businesses, and studio buildings like Thorpe, Northrup King, and the California Building. There are shuttle buses with brewery, pottery, and history tours. What a great way to bridge cultures and age groups and to open possibilities for expression, growth and healing!

THE ETHNIC DANCE THEATRE
2337 Central Avenue Northeast

Vocal Ensemble in Bulgarian costume 1996.

The Ethnic Dance Theatre (EDT), since 1995, has had its home on the upper floors of the Latvian House on Central Avenue in the former Dover Hall. It is the only professional international dance company in the Upper Midwest and one of only five in the entire USA.[3]

An old-fashioned elevator leads to the third floor, where the performers rehearse and give small performances in a big hall with a creaky hardwood floor. But EDT has performed at the more elegant Orchestra Hall in Minneapolis, the Ordway Theater in St. Paul, and at St. Paul's Festival of Nations held at RiverCentre in St. Paul. In 1997, EDT began annual performances at the Minnesota Historical Society auditorium in St. Paul. It also presents more than 250 in-school programs a year, reaching over 8,000 students.

World Music and Dance

The company is dedicated to the artistic performance and preservation of world music, song, and dance. For the past 27 years, it has brought 55 different cultures and traditions to life in colorful and spellbinding performances. It has two additional connections to Northeast Minneapolis: Many of the dances are from Eastern Europe, but the range has been broadened to include Central Asia, Mexico, Central America, and the Middle East. In addition, five of the performers live in Northeast: Dee Langley, Royal Anderson, John Czichray, Jana Stow, and Daniel Wovcha.

There's a lot of stamping, whooping, and hollering going on when they perform, and the audience re-

sponds with a lot of vocal "accompaniment" and a boundless amount of spirit. The company even has a following of "groupies."

The Ethnic Dance company is made up of 40 professional dancers, musicians, and singers. The troupe members come from all parts of the Twin Cities. Several are from other countries. Three are from Bulgaria, two from the Czech Republic, and two of them are second-generation Ukrainian and Latvian. They range in age from the 20s to the 50s.

Many former EDT members work at a toy company in St. Paul called Beka, Inc., owned by Peter Kreisman, a 58-year-old grandfather, who retired from the Ethnic Dance Theatre after 25 years as a dancer.

Performing Croatian Harvest Dance in 2001.

[3]Some of this material is taken from the EDT web site www.ethnicdancetheatre.com. It is used here with permission of Joan Elwell.

Foundations

Donald LaCourse and Jonathan Frey founded the Ethnic Dance Theatre in 1974. It began as a small ensemble of dancers and singers presenting Balkan traditions. In the early 1980s, native guest dancers, choreographers, and musicians worked with the company to enlarge the cultural repertoire. They began to incorporate more live music into the performances, and by 1984, the EDT Folk Orchestra became a regular part of the performances.

The performers strive for authenticity and LaCourse takes international trips to research dance techniques and costumes, and to better understand the cultural context of the company's work. Each piece they perform is not merely a reproduction of a single folk dance or song, but rather a re-creation of the joy, history, and traditions of multiple cultures. EDT has a stunning collection of over 5,000 costume pieces from around the world, including hats, shoes, aprons, and scarves. Several local people make the costumes, which are duplicated from authentic designs and imported fabrics.

The driving force behind EDT, Don LaCourse, serves as artistic director, lead dancer, choreographer, and costume designer. He grew up in a family of German folk dancers. His brother, Mark, and sister, Renee, are also EDT members. When he was six years old, he saw a troupe of Slavic dancers, and from then on wanted to have a dance company of his own. He has been nationally recognized for his choreography and was commissioned to create a work for the Chimera Theater in Minneapolis. He has also worked with folk groups from Seattle and Los Angeles.

The Mila Vocal Ensemble and EDT Folk Orchestra both draw material from firsthand sources, field recordings, and rare songbooks. Mila sings in native languages and employs vocal techniques unique to each particular country or region. The orchestra specializes in Eastern European music, and in the summer of 2000, they performed at the prestigious Koprivshtista Festival in Bulgaria.

Natalie Nowytski has performed with EDT since 1996, and is the Mila Vocal Ensemble director. She also sings in the band, "Boris and Natasha," takes Taiko or Japanese drum lessons, plays the guitar and Bulgarian bagpipe, and makes jewelry and Ukrainian Easter eggs. Her soft spot for folk songs came from attending EDT performances at the age of eight.

International Instruments

The EDT Folk Orchestra showcases a broad array of instruments from countries all over the world, such as bagpipes, flutes, and a Turkish zurna, which is a double reed or a primitive oboe. They were voted Best Ethnic Ensemble by the Minnesota Music Academy and released its first CD in August of 2001.

When Dee Langley first played the accordion at the age of four, little did she know that her love for the instrument and her passion for music, would eventually reap numerous first-place honors, take her to Europe, and earn her several guest appearances with the Minnesota Orchestra and the St. Paul Chamber Orchestra. Dee has been a part of EDT since 1998, and has also performed with the Dolina Polish Folk Dancers. She is the chairperson for the Northeast Accordion Festival and the "squeezer" of Skweezergrabbit, a three-piece musical ensemble.

The troupe has toured throughout the Midwest and has traveled to Hungary, Bulgaria, and France. In 1987, the group was honored with the McKnight Excellence in the Arts Award, and in 1990, EDT received its first grant from the National Endowment for the Arts (NEA).

CALIFORNIA BUILDING AND MILL CITY COFFEE SHOP
2205 California Street Northeast

*Mill City Coffee Shop in the California Building
Photo taken in 2001.*

The California Building stands among small houses in a quiet neighborhood. It is a two-story brick complex next to a six-story building that was once a grain mill.

The dark aged brick and rustic tall windows are quite a contrast to the new cedar deck with a pergola (arbor) overhang that has been added to beautify the front of the building. The entrance is surrounded in summertime by morning glories that wrap around the steps, with bright red poppies and other wild flowers in wooden planters. And somehow it all blends together. It is a flourishing building with 75 units housing painters, sculptors, a man who makes wooden furniture by hand, a woman who arranges dried flowers, a piano tuner, and even a yoga instructor. There are several mixed media businesses which do video and computer design, picture framers, printmakers, and photographers. Creative artists who make ethnic beaded jewelry, quilts, abstract painted duvets, mosaics, ceramics, hand-made paper items, magnets, and candles have offices there too.

A Varied Past

The California Building began as a two-story bottle factory in 1915, then it became a grain mill from 1919 to 1935. After the St. Anthony Power Company began, it was no longer necessary to be right on the river to get power, and this mill was one of the first electrified mills. The mill was connected by skyways to the grain elevator. The freight trains came right into the building and dumped the grain into the chutes, where it was washed and processed into cereal.

From 1935 to 1975, the California Building became the home of Franklin Manufacturing Company, which was started by Guy Pugh. The original company made transformers and became the largest battery-charger company in the country. During World War II, it manufactured quartz crystals used in radio transmitting. Franklin also made giant chargers designed to operate under extremely cold climate conditions for the Russian front. After World War II, the company began manufacturing household appliances under the same name.

In 1962, the Studebaker Company purchased Franklin Manufacturing. In the late 1970s and into the 1980s, the California Building became a multiuse building, with numerous owners like O. Walter Johnson, who owned Connco Shoes, an organ maker, a few artists, and other small businesspeople. The St. Anthony Fraternal Order of Eagles was one of the main tenants in the 1970s and 1980s and it owned a large dance floor in the center of the building.

In 1991, Jennifer Young and John Kremer, who came from South Minneapolis, bought the building. They loved Northeast Minneapolis. It was perfect for artists, with lots of big windows, a view of Northeast, and roomy studios that had a nice loft feeling. The building was already filled with a hodgepodge of artists when the idea came to Young and Kremer, "Let's make this an arts center." The demolition of buildings in the Warehouse District in downtown Minneapolis, to make way for a Target Center Sports Arena, dislocated many artists, who needed a new home. The timing was perfect.

The new owners removed decades of flooring, four and five layers of carpeting and tile that revealed the original hardwood floors. They demolished and constructed walls on the first and second floors. They had new windows made and installed when they found out there were no windows in half of the sixth floor. The openings for the windows had been boarded up with plywood. They also found out that a fire in the 1970s had burned the Victoria Elevator Company on the corner of Twenty-third and California Street, which had been between the building and the grain silos.

A Gathering Place

In 1995, after renovation and the addition of a cedar deck, the Mill City Coffee Shop was born, named for the building's original use and Minneapolis's status as the former milling capital of the world. With comfortable vintage furniture, tables, an upright piano, and a bathroom that is located in an old elevator shaft, Mill City has become a popular place. Flavored coffee concoctions, fresh bakery goods, unique homemade soups, and sandwiches made to order are served on bright Fiestaware by efficient hosts. Friendly and colorful people blend with the ambience of an artist's building. The coffee shop has become a gathering place for artists. It also centered the arts community and connected them with the Sheridan and Bottineau neighborhoods.

John and Jennifer not only improved the building, they created a gathering place and made it work. Northeast became one of the first neighborhoods to adapt and reuse a historical building for the arts community.

MAIN STREET THEATER
1029 Northeast Main Street

A theater bombing, the fourth in Minneapolis within less than a year, destroyed the Main Street Theater at Broadway and Main Streets Northeast at 11:35 p.m. on May 19, 1926. The explosion occurred when the building was empty, but was of such force that it awakened residents within a radius of five blocks and blew out windows in two homes across the street. It brought 1,000 persons, many of them dressed in night clothes to the scene.[4]

Firefighters investigating the ruins stated they smelled the fumes of burned dynamite, but they were unable to find any parts of the bomb. The force of the explosion tore out the entire front of the one-story wood frame and stucco building, and wrecked the interior. Windows in the homes of Ray O'Leary, 1022 Main Street Northeast, and Ralph Selbert, 1024 Main Street Northeast, were broken by the blast.

The Main Street Theater bombing was one of a series of eight "bombing outrages" that had taken place at the home or property of employers during controversies with various labor unions. This was the fourth theater bombing in less than a year and each theater was on the "unfair" list of the Motion Picture Operators Union, although the Hennepin County grand jury was never able to prove that unions were responsible for the bombings.

[4]The account here is taken from the *Minneapolis Journal*; the *Minneapolis Tribune*, May 19, 1926; and from the book by William Millikan, *A Union Against Unions* (St. Paul: Minnesota Historical Society Press: 2001).

Pottery as a Pioneer Craft

Jim Brown forming a piece at his pottery wheel at 212 Pottery, photo taken in 2001.

The earliest earthenware plant in Minnesota was St. Anthony Pottery, established in 1857 by Louis Kampff and located on the river at Eighth and Marshall Street Northeast. (Red Wing Pottery was established in 1878.) Kampff had emigrated from Germany in 1854, and began making pottery in a log shanty. Behind the shanty was a clay pit where he obtained his raw material. In 1860, he erected a two-story building which became his pottery plant. This building was still in use as a residence by a family member as late as 1947.

Kampff had three employees and paid them $600 a year in 1859 and 1860. The pottery business annually produced earthenware valued at $1,000. The business grew and the company was producing $3,000 worth of pottery annually by 1870. In 1876, Kampff sold the business to Jonas G. Swahn. He and his son, Charles, manufactured flowerpots, garden vases, hanging baskets, and terra cotta work made to order. After Jonas Swahn died, it continued until 1904 as J. G. Swahn's Sons.

Two other pottery firms in Minneapolis during this time were John C. Malchow Company, established in the 1870s, and Jules Gobeaux, who operated a plant from 1895 to 1901. Malchow was said to have produced 100,000 flowerpots a year in the early 1880s. Barter was in common use at that time and many items such as produce were accepted in exchange for wares.

There are currently seven full-time pottery businesses in the Northeast area. They are listed here.

TWO-12 POTTERY
212 Thirteenth Avenue Northeast

Jim Brown is the master potter at Two-12 Pottery. Although he has been there for only two years, he has been making pottery for over 34 years. He is a studio or artist potter in the traditional sense. The pieces he forms on the potter's wheel are functional pottery made for serving food or for decorative use.

About 10 steps go into making a finished piece, and the process can take up to 30 days. The pottery is made one piece at a time and formed according to the tradition of the potter's wheel. The clay is formed, trimmed, and handles-if needed-are added. Then the piece is dried, fired, glazed, and refired. Mugs, casseroles, and vases are some of the more popular pieces. No two pieces are ever the same; each will have a slight variation which makes it a true work of art.

ADDITIONAL POTTERY BUSINESSES

- **Dock 6 Pottery**, 425 Wilson Street Northeast
- **Clay Squared to Infinity**, 2913 Central Avenue Northeast
- **MTL Studios**, 451 Taft Street Northeast
- **Nameless Wildness Clay Works**, 1800 Taylor Street Northeast
- **Sosin/Sosin Gallery**, 1231 Washington Street Northeast
- **Evla Pottery**, 912 University Avenue Northeast

The first family of Rhythmland, front row – Gary Gese, Peggy Gese, Don Gese.
Back row – Tony Gese, Judy Sowka, Karen Haverty, and Barbara Gese.
Photo taken on closing night June 30, 2001.

Rhythmland Closes

1835 Central Avenue Northeast

Rhythmland Rink on Central Avenue, 1960's.

Rhythmland was one of the most recognized landmarks of Northeast Minneapolis. Just about every child who grew up in Northeast experienced the sheer joy, and sometimes first-time fear, of flying around the roller rink at one time or another. Whether for a friend's birthday party, a little pre-adolescent flirting, or meeting the man or woman of their dreams, generations of Northeast residents flocked to this local hotspot. Likewise, when you ask someone from another part of town if they've ever been Northeast, the most likely response is, "Sure, I skated at Rhythmland when I was young."

Beginnings

Don and Peggy Gese purchased the roller rink from Oscar and Clyde Beck in 1958. At that time it was called Ordemann's Roller Rink. Owned by Mom and Pop Ordemann, their son Henry took it over in 1946.

Don started working at the rink when he was in his early twenties. He worked as a floor guard and kept the rink traffic at an even pace. He ruled the floor, you might say. He had been skating ever since he was a six-year-old growing up in Grand Forks, North Dakota.

Don and Peggy changed the name to Rhythmland in the 1960s. After the Minneapolis Arena and the North Side Roller Rink closed in 1956, it was the only roller rink in the city limits for a while and kids came from all over.

At first, they rented out metal skates that clamped onto your shoes. Skaters wore a key around their neck

Owners Don and Peggy Gese in 2001 and in the 1950's.

63

that was used for adjusting the size of the skates. Not many people owned their own skates back then. Early skates had wooden wheels and made a whirring sound when they wore off unevenly. Recorded organ music that was made for dance skating was played.

Glen Livingston started giving dance skating lessons in 1956. He stayed there for over 40 years. Some of the favorites were waltzes, the two-step, and the fourteen-step. The Tango Waltz was also very popular. There were special skate times for couples and trios. There was always a group of "wallflowers" who watched from the sidelines.

Enlarging and Enhancing Rhythmland

In the 1970s, Gese built a 20-foot addition onto the north end of the building. He replaced the dark green plywood floor with a trap door that went down to the cellar. These trap doors were common in old homes in Northeast Minneapolis. The new floor came from the Minneapolis Arena, on Dupont Avenue South, which had closed in 1966. Gese also added a concession stand and game room. The rink at Rhythmland was complete with strobe lights and three-mirrored balls. Rhythmland was the first to hold competitions. The winners went on to regionals and then nationals.

The Gese family all helped to run the rink-Gary Gese, Barbara Gese, Tony Gese, Judy Gese Sowka, and Karen Gese Haverty, as well as Don and Peggy. The boys worked as DJs, and the girls at the snack bar and skate counter. Karen says she loved to watch her parents skating together. Just the two of them side by side made a picture of grace and elegance.

When their parents wanted to retire and were thinking of selling the rink, daughters Barbara Gese and Karen Haverty bought the place in 1988 and ran it until it closed.

Rhythmland was generous and gave back to the community. In the 1970s and 1980s, Rhythmland took part in the Jerry Lewis telethon. They also sponsored and coached Special Olympic teams for the final 12 years.

Bob Vangene and Don Gese had a routine where they would do synchronized skating. They would skate backwards perfectly. The joke was they had two fingers locked to each other. Bob hung out there in the 1960s and 1970s.

Ghosts of the Past

I was privileged enough to be included in Rhythmland's final skate on June 30, 2001. After 40 years of owning the rink, Don and Peggy Gese and their family were closing down. Times had changed and it was time to move on. It was a bittersweet night for the friends, family, and longtime patrons of Rhythmland. A group of people came to say goodbye to their old hangout and share some of their treasured memories.

Just walking through the place that night made me feel the spirits of those who fell in love at Rhythmland. So many people laughed and cried and loved and lost under the mirrored glass disco ball that still hung over the middle of the rink. And the multicolored lights that provided the atmosphere of romance were still there. I could almost hear the ghosts of the past as I walked toward the skate racks for the last time–"What size, ma'am?" "Tuck the laces in, please," then the chunk, chunk sound of skates being put back in the racks. That was back in the "good ole days" when everyone wore skates, when the creator of inline skates was still a young tyke.

I smelled the popcorn and thought of the generations of teenagers who skated here. As I walked by the bathroom I could almost hear the voice of a young ingenue zooming in, saying "Oh my gawd!! I just skated with Rich, he is such a hunk!" I remembered the constant humidity on the walls, the smell of leather skates and the disinfectant that was sprayed in them after each use.

Some Fine Romances

Evelyn Wilson met her husband at Rhythmland. She skated seven days a week in the 1940s. She says it was not unusual for people to meet the one they would marry at Rhythmland, because there were so many to choose from and they were there so often. She thinks there were about 50 couples she knows of that met each other there and eventually got married. On the weekends she would work all day, go horseback riding at night with the gang, then skating at Rhythmland, then to Larry's or the Roadhouse for dancing, and finally bowling at Central Avenue Bowl on Twenty-fifth and Central. All in one day! She hung out with the same group of friends. They loved to do the Circle Waltz, Chicken Scratch, Dutch Roll, and Two Step.

Caroline Gage said it was her special hangout; everyone went there to meet up with their friends. She started skating at Rhythmland in 1948. They'd skate first on Saturday nights, then they'd go out to Ron Clare's or the Crest Cafe, then off to Central Avenue Bowling Alley, and back to skate again. She met her husband, Ron Gage, during a "Ladies Choice" waltz. When she asked him to dance, his friend said, "He doesn't skate with girls." He was pretty shy, but didn't refuse. A week later they were going steady. One of their favorites was the "Blue Skirt Waltz." Caroline also introduced Don Gese to his wife, Peggy. She and Peggy are still good friends. They hung out with a group of about 20 friends who met at the rink each week.

Some others from their group were Ron Benson, who used to work there in the early 1950s and skated six days a week. He remembers 30 or 40 people out on the floor doing the "Dutch Roll." Some of the favorite songs were "Peggy Sue" and "Henry the Eighth." The "Midnight Waltz" was always a great closer. Ron still skates two or three times a week with the Metro Skate club and the Roller Roamers.

Bonnie Iacarella met her husband, Jay, at Rhythmland, too. They skated in the 1950s and 1960s. He helped to run the place on weekends and would stay and skate after the last session, which was about midnight. Their group used to have "Hard-Time Costume Parties," where everyone would dress in rags. Their group's favorite skate dances were the Limbo, Chicken Scratch, Lindey, Coliseum, and the Tango.

Halloween party 1952

There was a shortage of money but never a shortage of fun. It was the era of jalopies, lunch counters, and dancing the jitterbug. The young people of Northeast and throughout the city hung out at roller rinks. It was a place to meet up with your friends, have a nickel Coke, unwind after a hard week, and maybe, with a little luck, even spark a romance.

The 1950s skaters had a style all their own. White socks and gray saddle shoes or white bucks, the Lana Turner angora sweaters with detachable collars, quilted circle skirts with stiff crinolines underneath, were the in things. On Friday nights, the girls starched their crinolines and laid them out for Saturday. Then on Saturday afternoons a mass of kids zoomed to freedom on their roller skates, and not so incidentally made their first social encounters with the opposite sex. For a couple of hours each week, more if they were lucky, the young teens shed the watchful eyes of parents and roller skated furiously to a rock and roll beat. Parents meanwhile were relatively certain that there was surrogate parental supervision not usually found where youngsters prefer to congregate.

Guys wore khaki pants and plaid shirts. Songs that were popular for skating were "Peg O' My Heart," "Sentimental Journey," "Dance with Me, Henry," "You Ain't Nothing But a Houndog"-the Billy Holiday version-and the "Choo Choo Boogie."

During the 1970s, tee shirts and jeans replaced those polyester styles of the 1960s. For skaters who grew up at the rink, there are so many "moment songs" that recall some special moment during their lives. "Sugar Shack," "Kansas City," and "Some Kind of Wonderful," with their perfect beats were good for two-stepping. "Surfing USA" makes me think of doing the "surf," where three people would get in a line holding each other's waist and surf around the rink. There was also the conga, which had a one-two-three kick theme to it, and crack the whip, where a long line was formed and the one on the end was whipped around the rink.

But best of all are the couple's songs like "Me and Mrs. Jones" and "Mandy," which was a favorite of couples' skaters, and the songs like "McArthur Park" and "Stairway to Heaven," which were longer so they were perfect for multiplying couples, otherwise known as the snowball. This was a ritual where a boy and girl would be picked to start skating together as the boys watched from one wall and the girls from the other. When the skate guard blew the whistle, the couple split up and chose someone else to skate with from the wall. This continued for several songs until almost everyone was skating with someone or had just given up and slunk off the rink to watch from the sidelines.

For many kids, the skating rink was the one place they belonged. These were the rink rats. Looking back the term sounds so derogatory, but at the time no one minded it. The rink was a place kids could come to shine, showing off their kick turns and ability to spin. The manager and his wife did so much more than balance the books and keep the place clean. They were surrogate parents to a generation of skaters, acting as confidantes, counselors, and friends.

Changes

Skating changed a lot over the years, the price of admission being one of them. Three sessions of skating in the 1950s cost 75 cents for Friday, Saturday, and Sunday, plus skate rental, which was 25 cents and 50 cents for an extra skate session. Skating in the year 2001 was $2.50 on Tuesday and Wednesday nights, $1 for Scouts in uniform. Wednesday was country and oldies night and Friday and Saturday nights were $5 and Sunday afternoon sessions $3.50 each.

As I talked to people on closing night, a common theme emerged: They would miss Rhythmland. It was a home away from home. It was farewell to a special place that would be missed. Closing night was a nostalgic affair and many people mentioned how they were sad to see it all end.

Some of the Regulars

This is dedicated with gratitude to Don and Peggy Gese and their family and all the skaters who made Rhythmland a special place and will keep it in their hearts. These were some of the regulars:

Donna Beck, Yvonne and Dick Brevig (also met at rink), Vicki Chesney, DeeDee Chesney, Tom Chesney (met wife Judy at Rhythmland), Patty Dietrich, Dulane Dougherty, Paul Ferstad, Bob Finn, Shirley Hinkel, Jerry Holmquist, Gene Herman, Marlys Hetland Herman and Donna Hetland, Curt, Al, and Roy Hafland. Judy Hebert, Gail Humphrey, Donna Konig, Betty Leske, Johnny Luthart and Betty Munson (they met at rink, married and had nine kids), Pam Conrad Martin, Dick Myers, Jerry Monahan, Pam Nistler, Ron Norton, Eddie Oulette, Steve Oulette, Tom Porter, Carole Palmquist, Tom Rundle, Elaine Stanek, Bobby Severson, Les Todd, Barb Herman Trebus, Judy Jackson Watson, Rosie Wells, Joannie and Bob Wells, Bruce Young, and Bill and Carole Young.

Rhythmland was so much a part of the Central Avenue landscape and a big part of many Twin Citians' lives. Don and Peggy were the best. They used to have a Christmas party at their house for anyone who skated at the rink and wanted to come. They loved people and had a special way with kids-strict but in a caring way. It was obvious they put their heart in their business. Rhythmland will be sadly missed.

A Night At Rhythmland

Hermann C. Burkhardt in 1935.

Quarries, Feedmills and Industry

BURKHARDT PLUMBING AND HEATING
1018 Main Street Northeast

Herman and Lilly's children taken behind the plumbing shop and home on 1018 Main Street NE. From left to right- Ed, Verna, Harold and Walt Burkhardt taken in 1918.

Burkhardt Plumbing and Heating was started in 1910 by Hermann C. Burkhardt, who came from Stuttgart, Germany, in 1890 at the age of two. His motto was "Right the first time." He didn't have his own wagon, so he took the streetcar to deliver laundry tubs, toilets, or whatever he had. The driver would stop and let him load everything up. Some passengers complained and some would get out and help. At that time, the streetcar charge was two cents, and Burkhardt was charged an additional penny because of his load.

Everyone in the neighborhood called him "the Chief." When Burkhardt went into the 1029 Bar, he would pick up a 300-pound boulder that stood outside the door. He would set it on top of the bar and say, "I'm not leaving until you give me a drink." He died in 1947, but his grandsons, Harold Burkhardt Jr., Gary Burkhardt and Chris Burkhardt still operate the business in New Brighton and Andover.

GRACO
88-11th Avenue Northeast

Forty year anniversary of Graco 1966

Once a quiet, family owned business, Graco has become a world leader in the manufacture of fluid-handling equipment and systems. The company celebrated its 75th anniversary in 2001, with a host of products its founders probably never imagined. Graco equipment squeezes tomato paste onto millions of frozen pizzas, pumps oil and lubricating fluids into millions of cars, spray paints homes, and helps give new cars their high-gloss finish.

Brothers Russell Gray and Leil Gray founded the company in 1926 with investors Harry Murphy, Sr., and Greer Wheaton. Russell Gray was working as a "greaser" in a parking lot greasing station when he figured there had to be a better way to lubricate cars than by using a hand-operated grease gun. Especially when the temperature had dropped down below freezing and grease was impossible to move. He devel-

One of Graco's first applications of the Model B greaser at 10th and Marquette 1926.

oped an air-operated high-pressure grease gun. After testing the invention and receiving favorable reports, the Grays established their own company with three employees. The fledgling company set up manufacturing and sales operations at 120 South Tenth Street in Minneapolis.

The Gray Company kept its employees working during the Great Depression. It expanded the product line and pioneered a traveling equipment display with a demonstration trailer. In 1931, the company introduced the "Red Head," which was a state-of-the-art, direct-from-the-drum lubrication pump. The Grays took their products on a number of successful cross-country tours, which increased sales and expanded distribution.

The company grew during that time and needed more space, so it moved to 60 Eleventh Avenue Northeast in 1938. During World War II, the company turned its production into helping the war effort and developed the famous Convoy Luber, which proved invaluable in keeping the Allied trucks, jeeps, tanks, and aircraft lubricated during the push through Europe and in the Pacific. The Lubers were loaded on rail cars and shipped overseas. With over 140 of Gray Company's men at war, women entered the Gray work force. During the war years, they earned two of the coveted Army and Navy "E" awards for efficiency in war production.

The Gray brothers opened a New York branch in 1944. After the war ended, management realized it could apply its fluid-handling expertise in many areas other than just automobile servicing. The product line was expanded to include industrial equipment for paint spraying and finishing, food handling, pressure cleaning walls, applying adhesives, and transferring inks.

With the death of Leil Gray in 1958, Harry A. Murphy, Sr., was named president. David A. Koch took over leadership of the company after Harry Murphy retired in 1962. The company expanded worldwide trade by creating an International Sales Division. Later, it established plants in Japan, Belgium, Germany, and France. It received the President's award for export excellence. Only four Minnesota firms have received this honor. In 1975, David Koch was instrumental in forming the Five Percent Club, a small group of Minnesota businesses that pledged to contribute 5 percent of pretax profits to nonprofit community causes. Today dozens of businesses have followed Koch's lead, and the idea spread to include more than 1,600 companies nationwide.

The company's name from 1926 to 1969 was Gray Company, Inc., and the brand name logo on the products has always been "Graco." In 1969, the company went public and changed the name to Graco Inc.

During the 1960s and 1970s, Graco products were being sold throughout the world. They were used to paint skyscrapers, fill aerosol containers, spray stripes on highways, coat candy, and apply urethane to aircraft. Graco's automatic airless spray guns applied adhesives between layers of foam rubber padding and turf at the Metrodome Sports Center in Minneapolis. Other products include Fast-Flo pumps used for de-icing airplanes, and foam insulation applicators. In 1980, Graco Robotics introduced its computer-controlled spraying robots, the most advanced automation technology for applying finishing and coating materials.

Russell Gray died in 1983. George Aristides was named president and chief executive officer (CEO) in 1996. That same year they opened a new manufacturing facility in Rogers. The company recently moved its corporate headquarters to the Technical Center in Northeast Minneapolis, and in 2001, Graco celebrated its 75th anniversary. About 20 to 30 of today's workforce are children and grandchildren of the original employees. Mike Tapsak, Burt Larson, and Charles Murphy are three of the original employees who started out at the downtown location and are known as the Tenth Street Gang. Graco continues to be very supportive of the Northeast community.

With over 140 of Gray Co's men at war, women entered the work force in 1940s.

R. A. Lohmar selling ties at Lohmar Clothing Company in the late 1930s.
Customer is Bertha Odegard of Central Norwest Bank.

LOHMAR CLOTHING
2337 Central Avenue Northeast

Lohmar Clothing was located in Dover Hall, next to Danielson Drugstore, and carried everything for men and boys except suits and shoes. First Communion clothes of white shirts and white pants for boys were popular items. It sold hundreds of Edison High School letter jackets to the teenage boys in the area.

Rudy Lohmar bought the store from Hy Gitleman on November 1, 1926, and changed its name to Lohmar Clothing. The Lohmar family had come to America from Lohmar, Germany, in the 1940s. Rudy was known for singing the German song, "Schnitzelbank." Before he bought the store, he had worked in a dry goods store in North Minneapolis.

Some of the employees were Vern Lindquist, Rush Bush, Bill Hanson, Jr., George Larson, John Ramstead, and Allen Humrickhouse.

Rudy's son, Bob Lohmar, started working at the store in 1960 when he was 16 years old. The store sold such brands as Arrow, Van Heusen, Jockey, Munsingwear, Field and Stream, Asher, and Pendleton.

Rudy Lohmar was active in St. Charles Borromeo Church. He once organized a group of people to build a house for a woman who had lost her husband and had been left with three children and no insurance.

Rudy worked at the store every day until shortly before he died in 1976 at age 77. His son, Bob Lohmar, closed the store in 1992.

Very few businesses remain in one family for 66 years. The success of the store peaked in the days before shopping centers, although the St. Anthony and Apache Mall offered little competition. The Dales hurt the business eventually. Lohmar's was virtually the last family owned men's store in Minneapolis and St. Paul. Twenty years before, there were probably 80 to 100. The building is now owned by the Latvian House.

NORTHEAST FEED MILL
1428 Marshall Street Northeast

Truck across Marshall Street, Bud Schroeder was the semi driver 1961.

Northeast Feed Mill was a landmark on Marshall Street for over 90 years. John A. Schroeder, a cooper from Germany, bought into the mill in the 1880s and incorporated it in 1894. The Schroeder brothers-Art, Joe, John, and Donald-ran the mill.

Located on the Mississippi River between the Grain Belt and Gluek's breweries, the complex included an office, warehouse, and the huge mill, which was 300 feet along Marshall Street. In earlier times, a pet hospital and Christmann Sausage were right across the street, prompting bad jokes about the association of the two businesses.

Bob Schroeder, grandson of the original owner and the last member of the family to work at the mill, says, "Whenever I mention Northeast Feed Mill, people seem to get excited. They like to tell about picking up spilled grain on the railroad tracks when they were little kids. Or they remember going in and weighing themselves on the huge platform scale. The big dial

Driver of feed truck is Nick Mueller 1890s.

E. J. Gulden (cousin), John A. Schroeder (grandfather), Frank Riedel (cousin) 1890s.

was about three to four feet across. A few people from the area came in and weighed themselves every day. One time the whole sixth grade basketball team from Holland School got on the scale together."

In the 1920s and early 1930s, the business became strictly wholesale, including distributing products similar to those manufactured by Purina and Cargill-mainly corn, barley, and oats. These grain products were formulated to feed cows, turkeys, and chickens. A wholesale price list of about 90 items came out each week. Cloverleaf and Northland Farm and Creamery were two of Northeast Feed Mill's biggest customers. It also sold a great deal of crimped oats, hay, and horse feed.

The Northern Pacific Railroad tracks ran behind the main building. Engine-pulled boxcars came in and unloaded grain into a pit, which was sent up a conveyer belt, weighed, and dropped into a bin. It was then converted into feed.

A diesel engine made electricity for many years, and allowed one-third of the building to be run by its own power. About 12 to 15 people were employed in the mill and warehouse, including Andrew Brezny and Sam Korba, who worked there for years. David N. Carlson ran the office. Aunt Mamie Heiges, a sister of Art, Joe, John, and Donald Schroeder, worked in accounts payable. She was well liked and never without a smile.

Northeast Feed Mill served mainly country people-primarily farmers who brought their livestock into the cities. Bob Schroeder got to know them and liked kidding around with them. Everyone was named "Elmer" or "Agnes" because he couldn't remember names. Leonard Kaminski and his brother from Silver Lake came in frequently. Customers would call up and would say, "This is Elmer," leaving the person at the other end to figure out which one.

Bob's father, John, was the mill superintendent and vice president of the company, and worked hard all his life, even in his later years. He would weigh in the feed at the top of the elevator, a metal-clad building, or he would be tinkering around and repairing something. Whenever he was up in the top of the mill working way too hard, Bob would holler up, "Hunisch, the sheriff is looking for you!" That meant: Go in and take a shower, put on some fresh clothes, and we'll go down to watch a ball game at the Met.

OLD QUARRY
Eighteenth Avenue and Johnson

When nature was handing out gifts to the East side, it sprinkled a lot of deposits of stone, clay, and rich brick-sand. Fine limestone crops were found along the Mississippi River and other parts of the city, but the majority of the quarrying took place on the city's East side. The stone and brick were used to make many buildings on both sides of the river. Blue, yellow, and gray limestone, used in blocks in the construction of many of the city's early buildings, lay only a few feet below the surface in Northeast Minneapolis.

Quarrying took place in the early years of the twentieth century in an area stretching from Central Avenue almost to Hayes Street between Thirteenth and Eighteenth avenues. Nicollet Island and a four-square-block area near Main Street and First Avenue Northeast were also quarried, according to Tim Fuehrer in an article in Northeaster, October 17, 1990.

If a shopper occasionally feels a little shiver at the Quarry Shopping Center, it may be because of that site's unhappy history. According to Fuehrer, over approximately 20 years until 1929, "20 people had died, including six children, in Northeast quarry accidents, and residents and the city council battled all the way to the Minnesota Supreme Court to control quarry activities." Many parents warned their children never to swim in the quarry but many did-and several drowned there. Fourteen quarry workers also died there.

At first, the quarry seemed to pose no problems. According to a Minneapolis Journal article of March 29, 1914: "Several firms have taken advantage of the great stone deposits in East Minneapolis and have equipped quarries with stone crushers. . . . The stone industry is one of the big ones on the East side. Hundreds of men and teams are employed in the district between Central Avenue and Johnson Street."

But as the city grew and more homes were built near the quarries, problems erupted. Residents opposed the

Landers Norbloom Christian Company owned a quarry on 17th and Johnson Street NE-1956.

quarry operations, especially, the stone crushing and blasting that caused "so much damage to residences it has made some homes almost valueless," according to an April 13, 1916 Minneapolis Tribune article. "The dishes jumped from shelf to shelf in the pantry when the blasting began in the morning, and rattled all day, due to the blasting." Soot was so pervasive that one mother claimed she washed her children's faces at night and she hardly recognized them for the dirt when they came downstairs in the morning.

By 1916, and continuing for more than 10 years, residents filed a series of lawsuits against the quarry companies. Local resident Martin Brede filed a suit to stop the Minnesota Crushed Stone Company (later the Gopher Stone Company) at Fifteenth Avenue and Johnston Street from continuing operations. It was first dismissed, then another judge took over proceedings, in which, in 1919, Brede and about 30 other residents won the case-after portions of the trial were moved to the quarry site. Quarry owners appealed the decision all the way to the Minnesota Supreme Court, which upheld the lower court. The residents prevailed again in a second trial, in which 19 plaintiffs won damages totaling $10,067 in July of 1921. The quarry was closed, and the city drafted an ordinance prohibiting quarry operations. But less than a year later, Henry Meyers filed a petition that the city's ordinance prohibition of quarries was "unvalid." Meyers won, and the quarry resumed operations.

By 1928, the only quarry operating was Gopher Stone on Johnson Street. But in addition to the blasting, noise, and dirt, the area residents claimed the quarries-working and abandoned-were dangerous. Unfortunately, their claims were borne out when nine-year-old Hugo Roos was walking around the rim of the water-filled abandoned quarry. He slipped and fell and drowned in 20 feet of water on April 10, 1928.

State Senator Lewis Duemke told concerned Edison High School parents that Roos was the sixth drowning victim in the quarry area in the previous eight years. The Minneapolis Tribune called it the "Death Quarry," and the Minneapolis Journal referred to it as the "Death Pool."

Residents wanted a fence built, but the city said it had no right to do so. The Edison High School PTA tried to have a fence built, but the city attorney responded: "The city or any other person has no right to fence the abandoned stone quarry," according to the April 18 Journal, "because it is private property." No one, however, was sure who the owner was; tax records showed a three-year delinquency. The Edison PTA first tried to have a fence erected and put a lien on the property, but no one would do the work. Finally, they raised $650 for putting up a fence through

a benefit dance. Then the owner of the property was discovered to be Gopher Stone Company. Rudolph Roos, the boy's father, sued the company for his son's death, but lost.

Its history of tragedy continued into the 1930s, when Raymond Kopczeski lost his eye in a firecracker

Quarry 1956.

accident at the quarry, an incident that eventually played a part in banning all fireworks in the state of Minnesota.

Gerald Magee, Raymond Kopczeski, and the late George Wasilak lived near Twenty-second and Pierce Northeast in the 1930s. When they were barely in their teens, they swam at what they called BAB (bare-ass beach) at the Quarry, despite warnings from their parents. "My parents forbade me to swim there," Magee said. "I made sure I was dry before I went home. My mother used to pat down my clothes when I came in the door."

Magee said that when they swam there toward the

end of their swimming-hole days, a dumping area or landfill was slowly encroaching on the quarry. Within a few years, all quarries were filled except the operation at Fifteenth and Johnson, which continued until 1958 when quarry owners relocated to St. Louis Park and Shakopee.

It was a landfill after World War II until the land was cleaned up and the garbage buried in the early 1970s, when the Johnson Street Interchange that connected to Interstate 35W was built. Later, the Quarry was removed and the Quarry Shopping Center was built in October 1997.

UNION WELDING AND MACHINE COMPANY
1134 Central Avenue Northeast

Union Welding 1134 Central Avenue NE in 1999.

W. Markley and Gus Bowstrom started Imperial Welding in the old World Airflow building on Seventeenth and Central in 1917. Markley had roots in Varmland and Skåne, southern provinces in Sweden. Initially, their main business was farm equipment and machinery. Their two major products were Just Right Sheer Plow Sharpeners for farmers and Deep Well water pumps.

When the Minneapolis-St. Anthony area shifted from its role as a leading flour city to an industrial manufacturing center, Imperial's business became more centered on machinery repair. The company moved to Eleventh and Central Avenue and changed its name to Union Welding and Machine Company in about 1939. This was before the new Broadway and Central Avenue Bridge was built. The old bridge was made of concrete cribbing, the new one of steel. Union Welding is down by the railroad tracks, somewhat hidden below the bridge, and most people don't even realize it's there.

The building was a former lumber company and first-aid station. Each interior wall was made of a different type of wood, which the lumber company had used for display purposes. During World War I, the building served as an Aircraft Identification Center where surveillance of airplanes took place.

Union Welding's major accomplishments include helping build the original WCCO Radio tower in Coon Rapids, the Anoka Municipal Pool, and the Foshay Tower in Minneapolis. It also took part in constructing the Basilica of St. Mary of Minneapolis and the historic Broadway Bridge built in the 1940s. The bridge was later moved, by floating it down the Mississippi River on a barge, to Main Street in old St. Anthony, where it connects the mainland and Nicollet Island.

Today Thom Markley, grandson of the founder, is the proud owner of Union Welding. He remembers his grandfather, A.W. Markley, telling about when pioneer aviator Charles A. Lindbergh used to come in to the shop to work on the engines for his planes. Thom's dad, Dell W. Markley, was part of the first graduating class of Edison High School in 1925-26, and soon after he taught welding at Dunwoody Institute. In later years, Thom had the honor of being part of the first full-term class to finish Northeast Junior High in 1959.

Specializing in the rebuilding and repair of machinery, the Union owners and employees call themselves glorified blacksmiths, handling jobs ranging from the repair of a kid's bicycle to a 500-ton punch press and everything in between. People used to bring their meat grinders in for repair, back when they processed their own meats.

The business has continued over the last 80 years. A fire took half of the building in the late 1980s, but it has been rebuilt. The company motto is "Our wheels turn! When yours won't!" Most of the advertising is by word of mouth.

Longtime employees include foreman Pat Nerby, who has been with Union for 30 years, David Gustafson, employed for 26 years, and Chris Hannan, an employee for 16 years. Clyde James retired in 1997 after 42 years. Helen Semanko, a true Northeaster, started working as the company secretary after high school and later came back when she was married after working at a different place. She retired after 35 years.

WINES DEPARTMENT STORE
1701 Northeast Fourth Street

Wines was a homey store, the kind we all love to remember. It carried an assortment of clothing and articles for women, men, and children. Customers at Wines received owner Helen Gawlick's undivided attention, but she never tried to pressure customers; she was just genuinely willing to help. She enjoyed helping her customers find just what they wanted that made them look good. Trained to do alterations, she was fussy about how the clothes fit. If you selected something that didn't fit quite right, Mrs. Gawlick or her niece, Ceil Thomas, altered it free of charge. If you were in a hurry, they'd do it right away. Purchases were wrapped in brown paper tied with a string.

Helen took the store over from her brother, Fred Wines, in 1927. A former dressmaker, she ran the store alone as Helen Wines until she married in 1944 and became Helen Gawlick.

She started out with 98-cent wash dresses, known as housedresses. They were usually bright cotton pastels, of flowered or plaid fabric, with buttons down the front and pockets-the kind of dresses that women wore into the 1950s. Some fabric was as low as 10 cents a yard when Helen started in the business, and hats worn to match their little cotton dresses were a big item. Some women would wear these print dresses for everyday and to church. As hats started to become less popular, Helen added more sportswear and pantsuits. She kept the store open Monday through Saturday from 8:30 a.m. to 5:30 p.m.

A devout Catholic, she gave hundreds of pounds of her clothing to various missions over the years and she attended Mass every day at 6:30 a.m. The store was never open on Sunday. "We need that day of rest and we owe that to our Lord," she said.

Her merchandise tended to be a mixture of both old-fashioned and up-to-date items. She had plenty of nylons, garters, and girdles but also stocked pantyhose and little girl's tights. Shoes, gloves, jewelry, purses, lingerie, work gloves, men's wear, ties, and suspenders were regular stock. She also carried children's clothing, potholders, sheets, rugs, towels, zippers, thread, embroidery items, some fabrics, a few dolls, puzzles, and other toys. Aprons, handkerchiefs, and silk scarves were still stocked at Wines when they were hard to get anywhere else.

Located in a small brick building, Wines' immaculately clean floors were wooden with rubber runners. The merchandise was neatly displayed in oak cases and on racks. Helen's husband, Joseph Gawlick, an upholsterer, helped her improve the store and saw to it that she had more men's fashions available. After he died in 1964 she ran it alone for many years.

In an article in the Minneapolis Tribune, dated July 7, 1974, Helen told how a woman once called her early in the morning and said she had to be at a downtown convention by 9 a.m. and needed something to wear. Helen told her to come right down to the store, before regular opening time, and she would help her. They found an attractive dress, hemmed it, and then added jewelry. Thanks to Helen, the woman looked great and made it to the convention on time.

Another day, a bridesmaid came in just an hour before the wedding ceremony. Helen outfitted her too.

Then there was the woman who came in to buy two yards of cheesecloth and walked out with $200 worth of merchandise. She became a regular customer.

Helen remembered her first customer, a little girl who came in to buy her father a pair of underwear. Helen didn't want to sell it to her, so she sent her home. Then the little girl's mother called and said it was okay. Helen continued working until she was in her eighties and the store closed in 1974.

ZUNDE TAILOR SHOP

Edgar (Ed) Zunde could rip blind stitches, cut, sew, and press a pair of trousers in just 45 minutes-all this between answering the phone and helping customers. He could speak Latvian, Russian, German, and English. He had a little trouble with English and sometimes couldn't find the right word. But his booming laughter, enthusiasm, and wit made up for all of that.[5]

He was born in Riga, Latvia, where his father ran a tailor shop. "Our family was from Sweden. But my grandfather was a tailor for Nicholas II, the last czar before the revolution. He died in revolution times." Zunde told Dave Wood that he had wanted to be an engineer, but the Russians came in 1940, and then the Germans came and chased the Russians out. "The Russians, they came, and jing, jing, jing! They break the glass panels and take my dad's fabrics, and then

[5]This is taken in part from Dave Woods' article, "Latvian Tailor Outwears Life's Tougher Fabrics," *Minneapolis Star Tribune*, August 31, 1983.

they took all the machines, but one. That's Russian work for you. My dad wanted to fight them, but Joe the Polish tailor, said, don't fight to my dad. They got the guns."

Ed Zunde said, "The Germans liberated Latvia in 1941. They were rough on the Poles and the Baltic people, but at least the Germans didn't take your machines. They let you work."

The Russians did come back, but by then Zunde and his wife, Velta, and baby daughters, Zinta and Gunta, were shipped to Germany, where he worked at forced labor in a German tank factory. Then he worked in a bakery and later as an interpreter.

The family traveled from one displaced person camp to another for four years. Zunde did his first tailoring for pay when he made a pair of trousers for a fellow Latvian, who in return hauled the Zunde family's scanty belongings in his horse-pulled wagon to a new camp. Zunde didn't complain about the camps, because there was always work to do, and he ended up setting up a tailor shop to repair U.S. Third Army uniforms.

In 1949, a man by the name of Ray Petersine, who owned an incubator factory in Gettysburg, Ohio, needed help and went to the former Latvian Embassy in Washington and looked over the lists to select someone he might sponsor. He picked the Zunde family. Later they learned that he was impressed that Zunde listed himself as a tailor, and he liked their names-Edgar, Velta, Zinta, and Gunta Zunde. The family moved to Gettysburg, and Zunde worked for $40 a week installing insulation in chicken incubators.

One day while shopping in a fancy clothing store in nearby Greenville, one of Petersine's daughters over-heard the storeowner say he needed a tailor. She told him a DP (displaced person) who was a tailor worked for her father in the Petersine factory. The owner expressed interest, and she brought the news back to Gettysburg.

Zunde was reluctant to leave his benefactor, but Ray Petersine said to him, "Edgar, you want to work at your trade. This is a free country and you're free to go. What you can do for yourself, you better do for yourself." And then Petersine helped them move their things. "This still touches me," Zunde said as he brushed a bit of moisture from behind his glasses.

Zunde worked in Greenville for 10 years, and then made the big move to Minneapolis in 1961, after he visited it in 1958. "Here I like it. All these lakes and birch and spruce. It's like Latvia. And so many Latvians here. I could not believe." This time they didn't move in a wagon. He set up shop in an old house on 1126 University Avenue.

Life was good to him in America. He sang in the choir at the Latvian Church; he was active in the Boy Scouts and owned a log cabin up north. Behind him, in his sewing room, were boldly stroked watercolors of the mountainous forests of Latvia that he painted from his mind's eye.

The tailoring business isn't what it used to be. When he came to Minneapolis, there were three tailors and a boot shop in the neighborhood. He used to make suits from scratch, but there wasn't enough natural fabric around to make it worthwhile, so he kept busy altering clothes. Well-known judges and lawyers would buy used clothes and hire him to make them fit.

Alfred Anderson Community Grocery 1229 Main Street NE in 1927.

The Corner Grocery Stores

Shopping for groceries was an entirely different experience in the earlier part of the twentieth century. Grocery stores were often located at a corner on a residential street and looked very similar to the houses surrounding them. The corner store, typically made of brick or stone, was one or two stories and appeared on nearly every other block in parts of the Sheridan, Holland, Old St. Anthony, and Beltrami neighborhoods. In 1965, there were 80 commercial locations in operation. Today, many of them have been converted to residential or other non-retail uses. The upper floors of these buildings were usually occupied by owners or rented out as apartments.

ANDERSON'S GROCERY
2200 Northeast Fillmore

Oscar M. Anderson was a grocer for 67 years. He spent 63 of those years on Fillmore Street. At 82 years of age, he threw his customers into a panic by retiring.

Up until then, he still delivered. And whenever a customer paid the bill, he or she would receive a good-sized bag of fruit. Anderson lived above the store for 63 years.

In the earlier years, he spent his mornings driving out by horse and buggy to his customers to take orders. He'd return to the store at noon to fill the orders and then drive out again, delivering until 7 p.m. He was still using wooden fold-up grocery crates that are now collector's items.

In front of the store were open pickle, sauerkraut, and lutefisk barrels. Anderson kept string on spools hanging from the ceiling, and poles with grippers on the end to reach boxes on top shelves. He sold penny candy.

Glass-covered bins were filled with cookies. Anderson's daughter, Mrs. Doris Krez, helped him out until he retired at age 82 and closed the store in 1970. Even after he retired, he would get an occasional check from an ex-cookie swiper.

DUBIVSKY'S STORE
2001-Fifth Street Northeast

The sign on the door read Peter J. Dubivsky, but both Pete and Mary shared the responsibilities in the little ma and pa grocery store they owned for 43 years. Many children from the neighborhood knew the Dubivskys as Mary and Pete, and they came often to chat and buy candy and pop. The older people in the area enjoyed the convenience of picking up milk and bread. The Dubivskys were known for their generosity and service and had extended credit to many of their neighbors ever since they purchased the store.

Pete, who came from the former country of Czechoslovakia, bought the store from his aunt in 1928. He met Mary in 1922, while visiting his brother in New Jersey, and he worked there as a butcher. Until coming to Minneapolis in 1928, when they bought the store. He operated a butcher shop next door and had a barn behind the store where he kept his horse.

O. J. Hedean grocery was just off Central at 1901 Fillmore Street in 1906.

Store hours began at 5 a.m. and ended at 9 p.m. for many years. People had only primitive refrigeration (iceboxes) and would wait until the last minute to buy meat and produce. When refrigerators became cheaper and more available, people could shop less frequently and hours were shortened to 8 a.m. to 6 p.m.

Mary kept a 1930 ledger in which it read that cigarettes were 15 cents a pack, butter 35 cents a pound, a loaf of bread, 10 cents, a dozen eggs, 22 cents, and round steak was 28 cents a pound. In 1940, a 10-pound goose sold for $2.25, a 12-pound turkey for $3, and a 7-pound capon for $1.98.

Days were long and vacations were few. Mary visited relatives in New Jersey on occasion. The summer before he died, Pete visited his homeland and was able to visit with a sister he hadn't seen in 62 years. In spite of the long hours, he was active in the St. Peter and Paul Lodge, St. Mary's Library Club, the Veteran's Club, and the Russian-American Club, as well as the Northstar Barracks 2636, where he was a past commander, and American Legion Bearcat Post 504.

As members of St. Mary's Russian Orthodox Church, Mary and Pete often donated food for special events and made welfare baskets for American Legion distribution at holidays. Mary was always baking large hams for holidays, funerals, and showers. At Christmas and Easter, she would have as many as 30 hams to prepare.

When Pete died in 1971, Mary retired and closed the store two years later. As a final gesture to her customers, Mary postponed closing the store on June 29 as she had announced. So those to whom she extended credit could have another paycheck and more time to pay their bills. The store closing brought an end to an era in Northeast Minneapolis of ma and pa stores.

Former Jedlinski Store building in 2001.

JEDLINSKI AND SON
Thirtieth and California Street Northeast

Leon and Anna Jedlinski owned the Jedlinski and Son Grocery Store and Butcher Shop. In earlier times, they would fill the orders and deliver the groceries by horse and buggy. Times were tough, and they carried people on the books even though they knew the customers couldn't pay. The neighbors called him Jed or Mr. Jed.

Leon was known throughout the neighborhood for his Polish sausage, all made by hand. Their kids would chop the garlic and Leon would add the chopped pork and seasonings into a hand stuffer. In the 1920s and 1930s, Leon would deliver to the area on Thirty-fourth and Main near the tracks where "The Greeks" lived. Greek immigrants and their descendants, many of whom later owned Greek restaurants in Northeast Minneapolis, worked for the railroad and lived in boxcars, fixed up inside as a house. The Greeks traveled to other towns, but Northeast Minneapolis was their home base.

Leon took care of them almost as if they were family. The kids liked to go along on these deliveries because the customers would always give them a nickel. All of the Jedlinski family helped out in the store—Joseph, Dominic, Edmund, and Lillian. The grandkids liked to help too. They would weigh the two or three oranges or potatoes that people bought. In those early days, people had iceboxes so people went to the neighborhood store quite frequently. Some even went twice a day, for lunch and supper ingredients. The Jedlinskis also carried a big supply of penny candy. Since many of the candies were two and three for a penny, the kids in the neighborhood could get a good-sized sack for a nickel. Root Beer Barrels, licorice babies, Tootsie Rolls, and bubble gum were popular.

Delivery wagon and driver for the Central Provision Company at 125 Central Avenue NE. in 1908.

F. William Wachsmuth and son, George Wachsmuth at 2210 Marshall Street NE, 1920s.

Witt Food Center 1835 Central Avenue NE, one of six modern super markets in the city in 1940. Note-Salem Church in background.

Mom and pop Murphey in front of their store

THE MURPHEY MOM AND POP STORE
Twenty-second and Hayes

By Virginia L. Martin

Grandmother and Grandfather Murphey frame the entrance of the mom-and-pop grocery store they owned on Twenty-second and Hayes Street in Northeast Minneapolis in a 1929 photograph, one of only a handful ever taken of their stores. Through a window, polished apples in pyramids framed by crepe-paper streamers are visible. In another photograph, Grandma rests her hand on a metal Kemps Ice Cream stand. An awning with the name Murphy's Grocery borders still another picture. The name is misspelled. The members of the Murphey family have always been inordinately proud of the spelling of Murphey-with-an-E (M-U-R-P-H-E-Y). The spelling supposedly distinguishes them as Northern Irish and Protestant. But there's no e in the name in the awning. The manufacturer inadvertently left it out and offered Grandma and Grandpa a 15-percent discount if they'd take it as was. Grandma and Grandpa swallowed the e with their pride and took the flawed awning anyway.[6]

The Hayes Street shop was the first of two stores that my grandparents, Ralph Emerson Murphey and Nina Whiting Murphey, owned over an 11-year span in the 1920s and 1930s. They bought that first store, on Twenty-second and Hayes Street Northeast in Minneapolis, in 1925, and sold it in 1929. About a year later, in 1930, they bought a second store on France Avenue North in Robbinsdale, a quiet old suburb directly adjacent to Minneapolis, and managed it until 1937.

A mom-and-pop grocery store is remarkable for its very modesty and relative dearth of choices, compared to the sprawling supermarkets with their bewildering array of products that we know now. But if neighborhood stores were not supermarkets, neither were they the convenience stores of today dispensing emergency supplies of bread and milk, gas and coffee to go. In these simple stores, most people did all their grocery shopping, happy for their convenience.

Grocery shopping was an entirely different experience in the 1920s and 1930s from what it is today. Refrigeration and transportation would not transform America into a consumer society until after World War II. Most people had their own gardens and canned their own vegetables and fruits to last through the winter. In addition to the gleaming rows of sweet pickles and peaches, cellars usually held a cache of pota-

[6]This article was first published in *Hennepin History*, Fall 1992

toes, carrots, and apples. The concept of (and pride in) self-sufficiency lingered.

The stores were close at hand, and people in town walked to their neighborhood store to buy fresh supplies every day or two. The stores sold the basics: flour, sugar, milk, butter, canned goods, eggs, baking powder, dried beans and peas, rice, spices, hand and laundry soap (though some people still made their own), cereals, penny candy, vinegar, canned vegetables, cookies, bread, and milk. (Even into the 1950s, however, the dairy companies made regular house-to-house milk deliveries.)

Curtis, Merle and Keith Murphey get a donkey ride outside the store in the early 1920s.

My grandparents carried only processed and canned meats and cheeses (butcher shops sold fresh meat) and they sold beer and pop, kept cold, not by electricity but in a cooler filled with ice. Hand-packed ice cream, too, was kept rock hard by ice and rock salt poured around the big metal bulk containers. Cones were scooped out with a metal scoop that idled in a jar of water on a shelf above the ice cream.

There was little variety in fresh produce, even when it was in season: potatoes, onions, lettuce, tomatoes, apples, cucumbers and squash. "Hands" of bananas hung from the ceiling. Occasionally an exotic insect was found in the banana crate. My mother, Merle Murphey (now Martin), found what she took to be a tarantula in a banana crate one day. She put it in a jar and took it to her biology class at Edison High School. Nothing as dramatic as a tarantula, the teacher said, just an "Oriental cockroach."

Self-service was another notion whose time had not yet come. Grocery clerks fetched everything, usually as the customer read the items off a list. (Impulse buying had not yet become fertile sales ground for grocery marketers. Not much besides penny candy would have been available, anyway.) Packaged grocery items were stacked on shelves all the way to the ceiling and retrieved with long-handled pincers with flexible jaws.

Butcher paper for wrapping packages unrolled onto the counter from a black metal holder screwed to the counter; its companion, a big ball of string, unwound from its anchor on the ceiling. A scale sat on the counter, and the Murpheys made change from a till, not a register, in the Hayes Street store.

A typical mom and pop grocery store in the 1950s.

George Hart Building at 19th and Central Avenue in 1942.
Started in 1905 and was later ran by Ed and Jan Widseth.

Red Owl Grocery Store 404 East Hennepin Avenue in 1930.

Work and family life were not so clearly separated as they are today. The Murphey family lived in the quarters behind and above the grocery. A bell on the store door alerted my grandmother or grandfather to a customer if their dog, Duke, of nearly legendary watchdog qualities, had not already done so. (After the youngest Murphey was born in 1929, Duke positioned himself between her and anyone who came in, relaxing only when he recognized the customer.)

Grandma opened the store at 7:30 a.m. and minded it all day long. She often stood her ironing board in the doorway between the living quarters and the store, keeping one eye on each as she ironed her way through radio soap operas and the family laundry. Grandpa had a fulltime job as a shipping clerk at Northwestern Casket Company in Northeast Minneapolis. After a prompt 5:30 dinner that Grandma prepared in the interstices between customers, Grandpa took over. They seldom went any place in

Pa Murphey

the years they owned the stores. Grandma occasionally managed to get to the Congregational Church Cir-

cle, which met one night a month, while Grandpa took care of the store. She seldom got to church. Their social lives were centered in the store. Grandma had very few close friends at this time, but some customers came into the store to "jaw" with her, as she put it. She was a good listener and didn't gossip, and people often came in to pour out their troubles.

In the evening, my gregarious Irish grandfather reigned, talking and joshing with everyone who came in. A few neighborhood men dropped in nearly every night to talk. Grandpa had no off-sale beer license, but occasionally he and a neighbor had a beer together. They stepped over the sill into the living quarters, popped open the beers, and drank them down, oblivious to any family activity.

Grandpa tried to close the store at 9 p.m., but neighbors would bang on the back door after hours, begging him to sell them a loaf of bread or a pack of cigarettes. Grandpa usually did, and he finally acceded to the inevitable, extending the store hours to 10 p.m. For some customers, no hour was quite late enough. Every night when Grandpa cranked down the awning (down, not up, because someone had once flipped a burning cigarette into its folds-hence, the "Murphy" awning), neighbors across the street heard it as a "last call," and sent over a child for a single quart of milk.

Only once did the store close during regular hours, when Uncle Ray, Grandpa's brother, died. The store was closed for the morning, and a few of the younger Murphey children elected to hang around near the door to tell people the store would be open later.

Times were good when Grandma and Grandpa owned the Hayes Street store. They hired clerks to help, and Grandma always had a "hired gal" to help her clean and cook, usually a young woman from her hometown of Balaton, Minnesota, who had come to the cities to find work. But the seven Murphey children-five boys and two girls-were all, except the youngest daughter, pressed into service in one way or another. As the oldest (and for many years, the only) daughter, my mother Merle's main job, starting when she was not much more than a child herself, was to watch and play with whichever littler ones were around. But she knew her way around a till from an early age, and she and her brothers learned to sack groceries and make change as they learned, in school, their "times " and the names of the U.S. presidents.

Much of the food came in bulk, and the boys' jobs included taking bulk goods and repackaging them in smaller lots. A typical job, said one of the five sons, Curtis W Murphey, was to empty a 100-pound sack of potatoes on the basement floor, sort them out, put them in 16-pound sacks, periodically running up stairs to weigh them and make sure. Wayne E. Murphey to this day calls up the image of pouring vinegar from a big barrel into smaller containers whenever he smells vinegar. The boys scrubbed the old wide-planked wooden floors, kept the shelves filled, and emptied trash. Darrell E. Murphey said he was paid 50 cents a week to keep the canned good shelves full. Once, when he broached the subject of his pay to his father, Grandpa responded, "Well, Darrell, if you think you're being paid too much, we can remedy that."

Crime, although less pervasive and violent in the 1920s and 1930s, touched people's lives then, too. Grandpa was minding the Hayes Street store one day when a man came in and asked to buy a cigar.

Grandpa bent down to open the glass case, and when he straightened up, he was looking into the barrel of a gun. Behind the till was a small office with an eight-by-ten-inch window that looked into the store. That was where Grandma was. She had a gun in the office, and her son Curt said she probably knew how to use it. She had worked at the bank in Balaton before getting married, and each teller there was outfitted with a gun. But she dared not shoot; she could see two accomplices outside. The phone was in the office, but she knew she could be heard. She quietly moved toward the outside door to hail someone, but no one was in sight. A man who lived in an apartment upstairs happened to be looking out the window when the robbers appeared, and he came down with his loaded deer rifle, but he too was afraid to shoot. The robbers got away with all the cash, but no one was hurt.

Hayes Store with living quarters in back.

In 1929, Grandma and Grandpa sold the store and moved to a house on Taylor Street Northeast in Minneapolis. There were by this time four children, and Grandma probably expected to have more time to take care of the children and house. But the man who bought the grocery asked her to teach him the ropes, and suddenly she was working full time again. In 1930, the Murpheys bought another store, on Thirty-fifth and France in Robbinsdale.

As the Depression wore on, Grandma and Grandpa Murphey carried more and more credit on the books. Years later, old customers stopped Grandma on the street to give her five or ten dollars in payment of a bill. She was completely paid back, sometimes in "strange and wonderful ways." Once she was given a piece of property, and another time she received a diamond ring. She said that she never lost a penny by giving credit.

Grandma Murphey was really the business head, the one who managed the stores and kept them profitable. She had graduated from a two-year business course at Gustavus Adolphus College in St. Peter, Minnesota, as a young woman. She was also a natural marketer. For example, when the bulk candy got down to the last trayful, Grandma would package it into quarter-pound "grab bags" to sell for a penny a piece. At random, she would drop a penny into some of the sacks. Word got around the Pillsbury Elementary schoolyard in a hurry that Murphey's was selling penny grab bags and that some of them had a penny inside. The kids would buy the bags, and when they got one with a penny in it, they bought another bag of candy. Grandma never had stale candy.

Another big candy day was the day on which Lent ended. Lent was a serious religious observance, especially among the many Roman Catholics in Northeast Minneapolis. Candy was a common Lenten sacrifice for the children who saved their pennies for the Catholic missions in other countries. Since Lent ended on Saturday at noon on the day before Easter Sunday, the neighborhood kids would come over late on Saturday morning, buy their candy, and sit on the curb out front, waiting for the clock to strike 12 noon. Then they could eat their candy.

In 1937, the owner of the building of the France Avenue store decided that he needed it for his own use. Grandma and Grandpa bought a house on Shoreline Drive across from Crystal Lake in Robbinsdale, packed up the five younger children still at home, and left the grocery business for good.

But the grocery stores lived on in family lore and legend. Grandma and Grandpa operated the stores for only 11 of their nearly 50 years together. Yet the memories and experiences and lessons learned have endured. In 1977, the entire family put together a quilt for Grandma Murphey's birthday. It was made up of different-colored squares ("color coded" by each of the seven siblings), each square representing one of the Murpheys' descendants. The embroidered picture used to represent Grandma was an awning with the single word Grocery. There was no room for Murphey, but no one needed an explanation.

Virginia L. Martin, a former editor with the Minnesota Historical Society, is a freelance editor, writer, and researcher, and has had a number of articles published in journals such as Minnesota Law & Politics, Ramsey County History, Hennepin History, *and* Mpls St. Paul. *She has also edited many books, including the story of a house restoration,* A Small Yellow House, *by Helen M. White.*

Marjorie Wheeler and Mrs. M.M. Wheeler at 1200 Second Street NE, 1910.

Grandmother and Grandfather Wheeler in their store 1910.

ZAHURANEC GROCERY
1126 Northeast Second Street

George Zahuranec's neighborhood grocery store was his life. According to him, "You got to be part of the community, not just a businessman."[7]

Born in North Minneapolis, George spent 56 of his 58 years on the Northeast side. He started as a grocery stock boy in 1937 and bought his first store in 1951. It was not far from the Second Street store, which he bought in 1963.

His store was always special to the Northeast community. The demand in the neighborhood for poppyseed was high, few people ground their own, and most stores didn't carry it. So George began ordering poppyseed in bulk and grinding it himself. He shipped it to Albuquerque, New Mexico, and Pine City, Minnesota. It was not just the neighborhood people who bought his ground poppyseed; he even sent it as far as London. All of this earned him the title, the "Poppy Seed King." He also began packaging povidla, a prune filling for pastry.

To make folks feel at home, he piped in polka music on a stereo. Often people would start dancing right in the store. Although George's heritage was Czech, he spoke Polish, Slovak, and Ukrainian, and he understood Russian. "People would rather speak their own language," he said.

George was known for his good heart. He offered credit and ignored collecting the bill for a young married couple who didn't have enough money to pay. He taught the neighborhood kids how to shake hands and how to tie neckties. The little ones would stare at the candy jar until George would notice and give them a piece.

The store was a community meeting place, complete with a bulletin board on which were posted notices, such as "Babysitter Wanted," "Polish Language Classes," and "Holy Cross Annual Fall Festival."

George liked a little sign that he put up in his store: "Yesterday is a canceled check. Tomorrow is a promissory note. Today is ready cash-use it." He didn't deliver groceries on a regular basis. But when elderly people called on a blizzardy day, or any other day, for that matter, to tell George they couldn't get to the store, he delivered.

George always knew who was sick and who was getting married and who wasn't getting married, but should, and who was having tough times. He was the local information center.

After 40 years in the business, he sold his little corner grocery and retired in 1977. George, a bachelor all these years, was getting married. The bride was Anne Dargis, a woman he had known since he was in the Navy during World War II. Anne's husband had died and she and George got together again. He moved to Parma, Ohio, to be with his new wife. A going-away party was held at St. Cyril's Catholic Church at the corner of Thirteenth and Second Street Northeast. All his customers, employees, neighbors, and friends were invited. An elderly Russian born woman put it this way, "There are no Georges left any more. We are losing a man who loves."

[7]Information is from "Northeast Minneapolis Grocer George Zahuranec Quitting Business After 40 Years," *Minneapolis Tribune*, September 16, 1977.

Hardware Stores

Henry Murlowski Hardware store in about 1928

The old-fashioned hardware store was family owned and its owners and employees knew their customers by name. Often, they knew your family and where you lived, and even the kind of fuses your house needed. It was a more personal and friendly atmosphere with knowledgeable employees, not the Big Box Store owned by a big corporation-the new so-called "do-it-yourself store."

In a neighborhood hardware store, you could walk in and ask the person behind the counter for a nut or a bolt. He would pull out a drawer and say. "Is this what you want?" and hand it to you, so you wouldn't have to walk up and down the aisles or buy an assorted package. They cut glass to any size, threaded pipe, made keys, fixed lamps, did screen repair, window and patio door repair, supplied stems for faucets, and sold lawn mower parts and serviced them. They sold merchandise that ranged from bird feeders to model airplanes and trains.

NORTHEAST HARDWARE
Twenty-Eighth and Johnson

Northeast Hardware, two doors down from Johnson Street Pharmacy, was also home to two beloved cats. Ann Graham, who captained the rowing team at the University of Minnesota, was always there with advice solid enough to build a house upon. But all that changed. One day a giant red sign appeared in the Northeast Hardware window at the end of the summer of 1998, announcing 10 percent off everything in the store. In mid-September, it was 50 percent off, and soon the sign was small and simply read "Out of Business." A few blocks away, a huge mall had gone up called the Quarry. Sure, it's great to have these stores, but have we lost something along the way?

In the old days you could buy cow stanchions or dynamite at the local hardware store. At one time, the standard customer was a male, but now 50 percent are women. Some would bring in cookies or candy and send letters to the owner thanking them for special care. Funny hardware stories: Question: "Why won't my lawnmower work?" Answer: "You forgot to put gas in it." Or "The blade is upside down." One woman brought in her lawn mower for a tune up. "It just hasn't been working right," she said. After examining it carefully, when she returned to get the mower, the clerk handed her a bag and said, "Here's the reason." In the bag was a snake that the repairman had removed; it had been wrapped around the engine.

BILLMAN'S FURNITURE AND HARDWARE
2506 Central Avenue Northeast

Owned by John Billman, Sr., as a hardware store since 1927. His sons Dan, Sam, and Paul ran Billman's Hardware starting in the 1940s and later added a furniture line. Long-time employee "Red" Asplund worked for Billman's from 1930 to 1955 in shipping and as a sales clerk; his job included shoveling sidewalks. He later bought his own store in 1955 at Fortieth and Central Avenue, called AA Hardware. He owned it for 30 years until he retired and sold it.

In 1969, Billman's became Our Own Hardware, owned by John Bonhus and George Zachau. In 1979,

Billman's Furniture, Hardware and Funeral Chapel 1940.

it became Bonhus Hardware and Marine, and some said it was the biggest retail hardware business in Minneapolis. Bonhus promised to always provide the finest in bicycles, household items, lawnmowers, snowmobiles, and snowblowers. It handled Starcraft, Larson, Forrester, and Mercury Motors. Al Morelli also worked for Bonhus and joined as a partner in 1983. He owned the skate shop, which included a huge line of new and used skates and hockey equipment. Three years later he went out to Beisswinger's Hardware in New Brighton and has been there for 15 years. In 1986, Bonhus Hardware became Twin City Hardware and Marine, which supported a skate-sharpening and retail business. It closed in the 1990s.

Ad for Bonhus Marine in the Argus 1972.

EGLER AND ANDERSON
1903 Central Avenue Northeast

Egler and Anderson.

Louis Egler started in the harness business in 1899, and in 1905, bought the interest of O. E. Larson, who was in partnership in hardware with his brother-in-law, Almer Anderson. In 1949, Egler sold his interest to Almer Anderson and George Brabec, who operated it for many years. Joe Le Tacon purchased the business in 1961 and named it Central Avenue Hardware. Another owner was Robert P. Bauman. He sold it to Lyle Johnson in 1974 and it closed in 1986.

Downtown Gambles Store Grand Opening 1939.

GAMBLE-SKOGMO STORE
2410 Central Avenue Northeast

Bert Gamble and Phillip Skogmo started the Gamble-Skogmo Company when they bought out an automobile agency in Fergus Falls, Minnesota, in 1911, and the company was part of the Minneapolis scene starting in 1927.

A cyclone struck Fergus Falls and killed 50 people, including the owner of the local automobile dealer. Gamble and Skogmo took over the dealership and developed a finance plan through which cars could be purchased on monthly payments, a revolutionary concept. Later, they discovered they were making as much profit on their parts as on their car sales and with a lot less worry. In 1925, they opened the first Gamble store in St. Cloud, which featured auto supplies at mail-order prices, and established themselves as the "Friendly Store."

A new Gamble-Skogmo store opened at Twenty-fourth and Central on March 12, 1937. Sid Olson came from the Stillwater Gamble's to manage the Central Avenue store. At one time it was called Western Auto. During the World War II years, when automotive accessories and hardware became unavailable, the company bought up men's and women's clothing stores, and began selling clothing.

In 1958, the Gamble-Skogmo Company operated 300 company-owned stores and had 1,800 authorized Gamble dealers in 20 Midwestern states, with headquarters in Minneapolis. An unusual feature of the organization was its partnership operation with all of its employees. Every store manager, department head, and worker was a stockholder. The four major items carried by the stores were tires, batteries, paint, and radios, which were manufactured exclusively for their stores. They also sold accessories and a general merchandise line, which included everything from washboards to hinges for barn doors. Many Gamble stores also carried furniture, and some stores carried an extensive line of cosmetics.

By 1966, Gamble-Skogmo bought out the House of Fabrics, Holiday Travel, the Curtis Hotel, Red Owl, and Snyder's Drug. It also had a mail-order shopper service, which enabled buyers to purchase almost any item imaginable, from farm lighting plants to sewing machines and jewelry. The Gamble Store on Central closed in the early 1950s and became Fredin's Department Store. In 1960 it became H. J. Carlson Hardware.

Ad for Central Avenue Gambles in the Argus 1940s.

MURLOWSKI HARDWARE
357 Thirteenth Avenue Northeast (next to the Ritz Theater)

Henry and Clem Murlowski bought the business from Hugh Fitzpatrick in 1925. Henry's son, Charles, worked part time when he was 15 years old. He had the privilege of learning the hardware business from his older brother and three adults who had the combined experience of over a hundred years. He said there were CEOs at major corporations who accredited their experiences of working at Murlowski's Hardware Store as a big part of their success. He also remembers European immigrants who couldn't pronounce the items they wanted to purchase.

Kids loved the hardware store, especially at Christmas, when it sold Lionel trains, bicycles, cap guns,

Hardware Store when it was owned by Mr. Fitzgerald in 1910.

dolls, and Tinker Toys. Kitchenware like Corning Ware, Revere Ware, and Melmac were big selling items. Henry's sons, Charles and Michael, took over the business in 1975. They closed the store in 1990.

Murlowski family cousins in 1900.

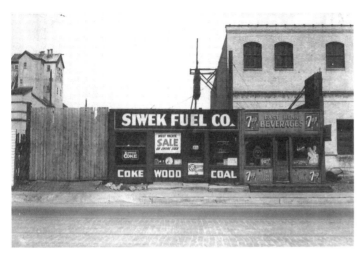

Siwek Fuel and Beverage Store 855 East Hennepin Avenue in 1942.

SIWEK LUMBER AND HARDWARE
2536 Marshall Street Northeast

Siwek's Lumber is one of the oldest family businesses remaining on Marshall Street. In 1933 the Siwek family began a coal and wood delivery service at 855 East Hennepin. In 1948, they moved to Marshall Street and built up their lumber operations, occasionally even constructing local buildings.

Two destructive fires occurred, in 1984 and 1993. On both occasions, the Siwek family completely rebuilt and even expanded the structures. A sawmill was added in 1990, and it is now known throughout the metro area for its specialized and custom millwork. The business is now operated by second- and third-generations-Joe and Judy Siwek, their sons Tom and David, and daughter Pat.

Siwek Fuel and Transfer truck 1939.

OTHER HARDWARE STORES

Some of the other hardware stores in Northeast Minneapolis are listed below.

Anton's Second Street Hardware, *2427 Northeast Second Street;* Owned by Joseph Anton, Jr., in 1968.

Johnson Street Hardware, *2207 Johnson Street*

Kampff-Warneke Store, *2201 Marshall Street Northeast;* Owned by Louis Kampff and his son-in-law, Edward Warneke. Started in 1927; in 1936, it was listed as a furniture store.

Mauren and Karow Hardware, *1019 Main Street Northeast;* Al Mauren was the hardware dealer while Bill Karow was primarily the gutter man.

Northeast Hardware, *2857 Johnson Street Northeast* Owned by Duffy family; it became Durand and Robinson Hardware.

Paulson Our Own Hardware, *204 East Hennepin Avenue*

Peter Wos Hardware, *1600 Northeast Fourth Street*

Rekuski Paint and Western Auto, *Eighteenth and Central;* Started as F and K Hardware, then changed to Western Auto. Owned by Jerry and Walt Rekuski.

Wasie Foundation

Stanley Wasie

For many young students, higher education would be just a dream if it were not for the Wasie Foundation. In 1966, Stanley Wasie, his wife, Marie, and their son, Donald, established a scholarship program for Minnesota students. Stan Wasie never had money for his own education. He was seven years old when he came from Poland to America with his parents. He was raised in Northeast Minneapolis on Sixteenth Avenue and Fourth Street. He knew what poverty meant, and by the time he was 13, he was earning his own living.

Stanley Wasie began his career with one delivery truck and became one of the transportation leaders of the country. He founded Merchant's Motor Freight, Inc. Later, he was chairman of the board of Murphy Motor Freight and state vice president of the American Trucking Association.

Those early years of struggling left an indelible mark on his life. Wasie believed America to be a great country for those who were willing to work hard and were not afraid to learn. He strongly believed in the importance of education and felt it a tragedy that anyone should be barred from learning because of lack of money. His heart went out to poor young people, so he established a scholarship program for those who shared his Polish-American heritage and wanted an education.

The Wasies were married at Holy Cross Church in 1925 and attended church there. They lived at Twenty-third Avenue and Fifth. The Wasies also had strong ties to All Saints Church. Later, they moved out to the Lake Nokomis area. After the death of her husband in the early 1980s, Marie Wasie devoted her time   and energy to the Wasie Foundation.

Children watching the fountain in Logan Park 1904.

4 Parks, Playgrounds, and Pageants

The parks have played an important role in the lives of both adults and children in Northeast Minneapolis for many years. Some of the activities have changed-the parks don't hold children's dance pageants any more, and roller blades and skateboarding may have replaced roller skates, but young children still make sand castles, swing, and slide in the playground, while older ones play baseball and football, or just "hang out," as they did 50 years ago.

Northeast Parks

AUDUBON PARK
1320 Twenty-ninth Avenue (Fillmore) Northeast

Audubon playground

Audubon Park was established in 1910 and named for John James Audubon (1780-1851 the great American ornithologist celebrated for his paintings of birds.) Audubon Park is part of a prairie restoration project, where native plants that grew here before it was a park can be seen. This way people can learn more about Minnesota's natural vegetation.

BELTRAMI PARK
1111 Summer Street Northeast

Beltrami Park was established in 1857 and named for Giacomo Beltrami, an Italian jurist, scholar and voyager who explored the most northern sources of the Mississippi with the Major Stephen Long expedition in 1823. There is a county and town in Minnesota as well as an island in Lake Agassiz named after him. Beltrami Park started as Maple Hill, a private cemetery where many Civil War veterans were buried. A monument in the park honoring Giacomo Beltrami was presented to the city of Minneapolis by the Minneapolitans of Italian descent in 1948. A dedication ceremony was sponsored by the Progressive Club of Minneapolis, a chapter of Unico National.

Beltrami Dedication Day 1973.

BOTTINEAU PARK
Twenty-second Avenue and Second Street Northeast

Bottineau Park was established in 1915 and named for Pierre Bottineau, the son of a French trader and an Ojibwe mother, who was born in the Red River settlement in 1817. Bottineau was engaged in the fur trade as scout and interpreter. A leader of the French-Canadian community, Bottineau founded St. Anthony, Osseo, and Red Lake Falls. He died in 1895 in Red Lake Falls. In 1849, Bottineau donated 14 lots for a church, which he named St.Anthony of Padua after the falls.

COLUMBIA PARK
3300 Central Avenue Northeast

Sliding on a toboggan at Columbia Park 1925.

Columbia was established in 1892 and named for the World's Columbian Exposition in Chicago in 1893, and its proximity to Columbia Heights. It started out as a 140-acre tract of hilly landscape. A three-hole golf course was completed in 1919 and expanded to nine holes in 1920. At that time, the cost of a round of golf was fifteen cents. A year-round Colonial design clubhouse called the Manor was added in 1925. In 1935, with the help of the Works Projects Administration (WPA), the course was converted from the old type sand course to a grass green and a complete hoseless sprinkling system was installed.

Group of women at a shoe race at Columbia Park in 1947.

DEMING PARK
Thirty-second and Fillmore Street

Established in 1924, Deming Park was named for Portius C. Deming, park commissioner and president of the Minneapolis Park Board from 1895 to 1899. Deming was a home developer in the Northeast area and sold lots just east of Twenty-ninth and Central. Many additions and subdivisions bear his name.

DICKMAN PARK
Seventh Avenue and Second Street Northeast

Established in 1949. No information has been found on the park to determine the origin of its name. It was renovated in 1991.

GLUEK PARK
Twenty-second and Marshall Street Northeast

Established in 1995, the park was named in honor of Arthur Gluek, former owner of Gluek's Brewery on 2200 Marshall Street Northeast. The Gluek's Brewery operated on this site for over a hundred years. The building was razed in 1966.

JACKSON SQUARE
Twenty-second and Jackson Street Northeast

Established in 1905, Jackson Square was named for the street on which it is located-which was named for Andrew Jackson, seventh president of the United States.

Jackson Square Field house in 1916.

Jackson Square Field house steps in 1916.

LOGAN PARK
690 Thirteenth Avenue (Monroe) Northeast

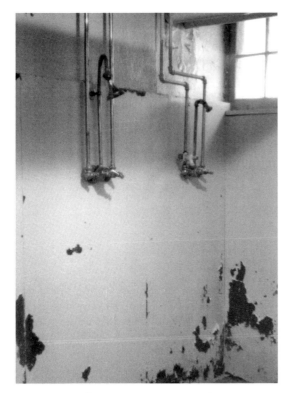

Showers at Logan Park

Girls playing broomball at Logan Park, 1940s.

Logan Park Exercise class, 1910

Northeast's oldest park, was originally called First Ward Park, and was established in 1883. The park was renamed for General John Alexander Logan, who was born in Jackson County, Illinois and died in Washington, D.C. in 1886. He was a member of Congress from Illinois, a general in the Civil War, a U. S. senator, and a candidate for vice president.

Marble game at Logan Park 1925. Note * Four churches on one block listed in the (Guiness Book of World Records) are in background on 13th and Monroe Street.

MARSHALL TERRACE
Twenty-seventh and Marshall Street Northeast

Field house of Marshall Terrace Park 1960s.

Established in 1914, this park was named for William R. Marshall, governor of Minnesota from 1866-70, who was "one of the best chief magistrates the state has ever had," according to Warren Upham's *Minnesota Place Names*. Marshall was also a lieutenant colonel of the Seventh Minnesota Regiment, served in the fight against the Dakota during the war of 1862. During the Civil War in the South he was named brigadier general in 1865.

Park instructors stayed as boarders in people's homes. Miss Evelyn Casey and Miss Mary Carlson 1929

Miss Casey, Miss Carlson, Vicky Koniar, and Marge Frenzel 1929.

Rosacker Pool 1941

NORTHEAST PARK AND ROSACKER POOL
1615 Pierce Street Northeast

Established in 1941, the pool was named for Hans Rosacker, a long-time florist in Northeast Minneapolis. He was also park commissioner for 22 years. His family still owns the florist business, which started in 1902 in Northeast Minneapolis. The park is shared with Putnam School and Eastside Neighborhood Services. Some of the activities include an after-school care program called Rec Plus. For teens, there is open

Cooking class at Northeast Park in 1972. Formerly known as the A Field for many generations.

gym, boys club and girls club, and the cooking class is very popular. There is a tiny tot playground, seven softball and baseball diamonds, football and soccer fields, and even horseshoe pits. Some people still call it the "A" Field or the Athletic Field.

WAITE PARK
1810 Thirty-fourth Avenue (Ulysses) Northeast

Playing volleyball at Waite Park in1953.

Established in 1949, this park was named for Judge Edward Foote Waite, a juvenile court judge for the Fourth Judicial District of Minnesota (1911-1921, 1931-1941). He was noted for his involvement in social welfare, civil rights, and civil liberties issues. Waite was credited with rewriting the Minnesota Children's code in 1940.

WINDOM PARK
2251 Northeast Hayes Street

Established in 1886, this park was originally known as Moulton Tract, but was renamed in 1893 for William Windom, a Minnesota representative in Congress. He was also a U.S. senator and secretary of the treasury for both President James Garfield and President Benjamin Harrison.

A chance to show off your bikes and buggies.

Children turn out for Wheel Day at Windom Park in the 1960s.

Wheel Day Parade

Note* For more information on parks see *Heart and Hard Work: Memories of "Nordeast" Minneapolis* by Genny Kieley.

116

Van the Cop-Park Policeman

Van joined the Park Police in 1910.

Back in the 1950s, if some folks had gotten their way, Logan Park would have been named Van Ruden Park. John Van Ruden was the park policeman for almost 30 years when he retired in 1940. To the hundreds of kids in Northeast Minneapolis who made Logan Park their home away from home, he was much more than a park patrolman. He was a symbol of kindness and protection, their guardian angel. Whenever he came into sight, children would stop their play to shout out a cheery, "Hi Van!" Van would smile. Some of their fathers and mothers did the same thing 30 years before.[1]

[1]The information on Van the Cop is based on articles given to me by Irene Van Ruden Trench (John Van Ruden's daughter); the *East Minneapolis Argus,* October. 30, 1952; the *Northeaster,* December 21, 1994; and undated *Minneapolis Journal* articles from the 1940s and from 1956. Copies of these articles are in the possession of the author.

Officer Van Ruden was sought out by young and old in trouble. He understood human nature, which enabled him to solve neighborhood difficulties. Neighbors admired and loved him, and they found a sincere friend in him. His genuine and gentlemanly qualities

Van and the boys. Van wears a real fancy hat in the 1930s.

instilled a sense of community in all the kids who played at the park and to all who knew him. He was a man who would give a helping hand, sponsor team athletics, as well as be their friend.

Van Ruden helped kids tighten the clamps on their roller skates (no one owned shoe skates in those days), helped boys on his beat shovel snow from the ice rink to play hockey, and picked them up when they fell and hurt themselves.

Van was not only policeman, but also janitor, care-taker of the grounds, and in his off hours, cleaner and water carrier for the skating rink. Football-hungry kids, forbidden the gridiron by their parents, gave their uniforms to Van. He hid them until game time.

Playing football at Logan Park. Van is the coach. 1930s.

Van Ruden had a way of easing things when tension-packed incidents occurred. Those who knew him said he stopped fights before they started, and many a young fellow who had one or two too many could thank him for being delivered to his parents instead of to jail in a paddy wagon.

Van also had a reputation with musicians throughout the city for the way he handled crowds attending band concerts and community sings almost every night during the summer at Logan Park and Bottineau Field. Each year the entertainers presented him with a token of their appreciation.

Van standing next to Logan field house 1930s.

His Way of Discipline

In those days, the park—not cars, movies, or the mall—was the center of a young person's existence. Those who got out of line at Logan were likely admonished with a sharp, "Cut it out-Van won't like it," and the trouble stopped.

The Logan Park Fieldhouse had shower facilities in both the girl's and boy's quarters. This was a great luxury as well as a necessity because not everyone had bathtubs or showers at home. The "Saturday Night Shower at Logan" was a household phrase on Monroe Street. When one day two big rolls of shower tickets, at five cents a ticket, were missing at Logan Park. The Sergeant who caught him, "Probation for those young thieves."

"I'll give those whippersnappers my own probation," said Van, the park policeman. For two months, two sheepish young culprits took four baths a day at Logan, one for every ticket.

During another incident, "Hey!" screamed the fruit vendor as a pile disappeared from his stand and came around the corner on two short legs. "Come here, buddy," said the park cop to the young culprit. He came. "Stay out of the park for two weeks for that little trick." This was the worst punishment of all.

Athletics

Old Van helped to organize many championship teams in all sports at Logan. He pointed with pride at the Northeast boys who had made their mark at the University of Minnesota. "Without these lads the University wouldn't have any championship teams," Van said. And to back up this statement, he gave the names of Martin Rolek, Butch Nash, and a host of others. He could spot a real athlete a mile away.

The Buffalo Athletic Club was organized in 1913 at Logan Park as a football team and entered in the 95-pound division in the Park Board League. From 1913 to 1919, the group progressed from one division to another and was undefeated in both football and basketball. The basketball champions reigned from 1916 to 1919. Van watched over the group in their younger athlete days.

Retirement

In the fall of 1940, residents of the Logan Park community presented Van Ruden, who retired on September 1, with an easy chair and an autograph book containing signatures of several hundred persons who had known him at the park. He was praised in speech and song. But there was one gift that delighted him the most. It was a small plaque that read, simply, "To our dear friend and great pal Van, from his athletes of Logan Park, 1940." A newspaper article announced the retirement party and called him a pillar of strength for those dark hours in a youngster's life when things went wrong. More than 300 people attended the retirement party, where 66-year-old Van Ruden was called "a copper who wasn't a copper" by those who attended.

When he died in 1956 at age 81, local folks wanted to preserve his memory. Members of the Buffalo Athletic Club were the honorary pallbearers at his funeral. It was here that members of the club decided "Old Van" should not be forgotten and shortly after that began circulating a petition to change the name of Logan Park to Van Ruden Park. Even though the name change was unsuccessful, Van Ruden was clearly a much-adored figure. John Van Ruden, the knight of Logan Park for 30 years, the trainer, the confidant, the guardian, was the pal of every Northeast youngster.

Yardville...More than a Playground

When a White House Conference on Children and Youth was held in 1950, the United States Children's Bureau asked all national magazines to sponsor projects related to children. *McCall's* magazine took this to heart and began a project based on a special playground operating in Copenhagen, Denmark, under the name *Skrammel Legespladsen,* which means "used materials playground," or "salvaged things playground." The initiators of this experiment stocked a piece of land with lumber and tools and turned it over to children. The play was unstructured and the children could build whatever they wanted. The theory was that creative play would allow children to learn valuable lessons about life.[2]

The Search for "Middletown"

McCall's searched for a community site for their project. They needed a community that was a fair representative of "Middletown, USA," composed of various income and social levels. It also had to have lots of children and a large amount of playing space. After months of searching, the editors felt they had found the spot in Northeast Minneapolis for its ethnic and economic diversity. It had lots of children and not many playgrounds. The area had been growing rapidly since World War II with an influx of Eastern European refugees.

[2]Sources for this article are Gillian Judge, "More than Just a Playground," in *Hennepin History,* Summer 1990, and John Kord Lagemann, "Leave It to the Kids," *McCall's,* October 1950.

Jimmy Barry sawing a board 1950

120

Shacks under construction and houses behind on 3400 Pierce Street NE, 1949

Lucy Goldthwaite, one of the editors, found an empty block adjacent to the Edith Cavell Elementary School (which was scheduled to be torn down) on Thirty-fourth and Fillmore Streets. The lot was close to a government housing project and was causing discontent in the neighborhood. A settlement known as the "prefabs" was home to 167 families with a total of 700 children in less than four blocks. There was no safe place to play and children often congregated around the railroad tracks.

The Margaret Barry Settlement House was asked to administer the program and promote it in the community. Some neighbors were worried about the project. They were not in favor of the prefab homes in the first place and feared that this whole venture would lower property values. They also feared that tearing down Cavell School and constructing Waite Park School would be delayed.

McCall's was on a tight schedule with little time for building community support, so it went ahead with the program of "Young Yardville," as it was named. *McCall's* provided $15,500 for one year of operating expenses, to cover tools and building supplies, an on-site toilet, and electricity and gas for a central office. Three adults were hired as counselors and supervisors.

The community also contributed to the project. The Minneapolis Board of Education provided the land. The Department of Welfare lent a collapsible trailer, and the local Teamster's Union supplied the fence to surround the lot.

"The Yard" Opens

Young Yardville, called "The Yard" by the children, opened October 3, 1949. During after-school hours, the children poured in and on Saturdays, even packed lunches so that they could stay all day. The kids challenged each other to build the biggest shack in the shortest time. The initial stockpile of second-hand lumber disappeared quickly. The children took all they could carry and lined up at the office to check out tools. Some even hoarded tools in secret places. When all the supplies were used up, some of the children quarreled and raided other children's shacks for provisions. But after a while, they realized there was a better solution.

By the second day of the shortage, most of the youngsters banded together. Tools and nails came out of hiding and new groups had formed from once-stubborn individuals. New ideas for projects also popped up. By the time a fresh supply of lumber arrived, a community had been born. As long as a kid could pound a hammer, there was no longer any distinction between the prefab kids and the others from the neighborhood.

Learning to work with tools was a valuable lesson. But learning to cooperate with other people was even more valuable. It was just as the project organizers had hoped for. Some built small houses, and some

had doors, windows, and more than one room. Edward Traficante, age 11, and his older brother, George, built an eight-foot square shack with a door, a couple of windows, and a roof. They even dug into the ground, mixed cement in a wheelbarrow, and built a concrete basement. It was only three feet deep, but it was still a basement.

Carving a totem pole became a joint project 1950.

Some of the girls equipped their houses with furniture and curtains, and raked their yards. Others stretched their abilities to include two-story houses with gabled roofs. Without prompting, they were figuring out problems using arithmetic and other problem-solving skills. Jim Peterson studied the rafters of his family's attic and decided he had discovered the right angle for his own building. The children were so proud of their houses, some of which were two stories.

Adults and children were climbing into these small houses and enjoying each other's company. They were talking together and reading stories. In the beginning, it was hard for these children to share their hammers. But many ended up as friends after they built their clubhouses together.

Interest climbed when word got around that President Harry S. Truman was coming to inspect the

President Truman received a scroll from Edward Traficante. Seated in the car with Truman are Senator Hubert Humphrey and Governor Luther W. Youngdahl in 1949.

Yardville venture. National attention accompanied community pride and instilled a more positive attitude toward the project and its people when he came on November 3, 1949.

Yardville remained open during the winter months of 1949, but few children came out during the cold weather. In the spring, the children came again, but in fewer numbers. Although most of them were between the ages of nine and twelve, a few were as young as five and as old as sixteen. Of the 55 to 60 kids who came each day, about one-half were from the prefabs.

Waning Interest

Interest began to die down as other summer activities, such as baseball, became more prominent. Community opposition was building up, too. Children were climbing the fence to play in The Yard on Sundays, unsupervised and against their parent's wishes. There were reports of cigarette smoking and vandalism. Then one of the shacks was set on fire and the Fire Department had to be called. Shacks in various stages of construction littered the yard, and the residents whose houses faced Yardville began to complain even more about its unsightliness, saying it looked like a shantytown.

Despite community complaints, Yardville continued through the summer of 1950 and into the fall without any accidents or injuries except for a few bruised thumbs. Then Northeast Minneapolis was brought into the spotlight when it was featured in an eight-page McCall's cover story praising the role of The Yard in providing a safe place to play and in teaching children the value of teamwork. The article provided a step-by-step guide for communities wishing to start their own Yardville.

When Yardville closed for the winter of 1950 there were high hopes for it to reopen in the spring. But McCall's decided not to fund the program for another year. And the Community Chest committees concluded that although Yardville had proved valuable and worthwhile, other programs were doing the same type of thing. One drawback was the difficulty of showing its value on paper. Community leaders also believed that publicity had exaggerated the value of "The Yard."

This came as a blow to those who were involved in planning and running Yardville. They felt that it was one of the most creative and exciting things ever done for children. Never had there been a program that had so much to offer. It was a wonderful example of community spirit and bringing people together. Children learned to relate to each other, and the project also built relations between young people and adults.

This rare project had potential for a significant impact on the community. According to McCall's, children in the 1950s were growing up too fast in a world they were not prepared for. Sometimes radio, movies, TV, and even schools give kids all the answers without allowing them to discover problem-solving on their own. No-trespassing signs, barbed-wire fences, and heavy traffic remain. But empty lots to play in for adventure are a thing of the past.

Lining up at the office to check out tools 1950.

Patty Kellerman, Patty Iversen and Diane Koelfgen working on their shack 1950.

Logan Park Recitals and Pageants

Mermaids

There was a time when the Logan Park Little Girls' Dance Pageant was the highlight of the summer. Children who were fortunate enough to be a part of these performances cherish them as among the happiest of their childhood days.

In the Thursday afternoon class in Aesthetic Dancing at Logan Park in 1921, 102 little girls with anxious eyes turned to Mrs. Alice Dietz. They came from all parts of the city, and their ages ranged from three to eight. Each struggled valiantly to keep a short, right leg pointed straight out in front of her and a right arm curved gracefully over her head.

At the end of the summer lessons, they had their long-awaited reward, a beautiful pageant. The early pageants were staged in the Logan Park Fieldhouse. Admission was by ticket only, with the audience limited to the children and their parents on Tuesday nights. The public would then be admitted to Wednesday night's performance.

The 1921 "Weaver of Dreams," the fourth annual pageant, started at twilight and was set among the trees. Mrs. Dietz said of these pageants, "To the child, imaginary people and places are almost as real as actual people and places-and much more lovely. It was

Mrs. Dietz with group of girls 1920.

these imaginary lands with which all the children's pageants have dealt."

Mrs. Dietz began her park career conducting dance classes around tombstones in Maple Hill Cemetery back in 1917. A year later she conducted the first park

Anne Moerls dressed in peacock feathers for the Weaver of Dreams 1920s.

playground pageant at Logan Park. Before graduating from Central High School, Alice Dietz had begun her career as a child actress, starring in the 1906 traveling production of *Buster Brown,* a 1910 production of *Little Minister,* and a 1912 role as "Sassy Little" on the Orpheum Circuit in Gus Edwards' *School Days.* She also performed with Eddie Cantor and was a Red Cross worker during World War I.

The "Weaver of Dreams" opened with little sleepy heads streaming to the stage from all directions. Dressed in pajamas, they followed the sandman. Then out came the inhabitants of the woods. Anne Moerls came strutting through the gate in a gorgeous costume and proudly swaying a tail of peacock feathers. Inez Du Lac was the parrot, Leila Odegaard was the white dove, and Margaret Keschold was the blue jay. The owl was played by Helen Hoffwegan, a robin by Eleanor Modeen, and a mother bird by six-year-old Jean Johnson dressed in yellow crepe paper. Florence Johnson played the Weaver of Dreams. Her costume had golden wings flashing with 50 tiny red, white, and blue lights. When they return to Dreamland, Neptune's daughter (Ruth Evidon) was pulled in a seashell by 12 little gold fish. The most fantastic scene was when the little water babies rode in on big green mud turtles and red crabs whose eyes flashed and twinkled at the whim of the tiny rider, who hid a fountain pen flashlight in her hand.

Through the power of imagination and sheer hard work, Mrs. Dietz created flowers that sang, cats that talked, and trees that giggled. Youngster's imaginations were pulled and stretched by a little woman who had no children of her own. She loved to tell the stories about the things that went wrong during the pageant. Once, little Cinderella was supposed to say, "Let's go to the salon," and she said "saloon" instead. An overzealous mother once painted the tin soldiers trousers with radiator paint, and the soldiers were too stiff to march.

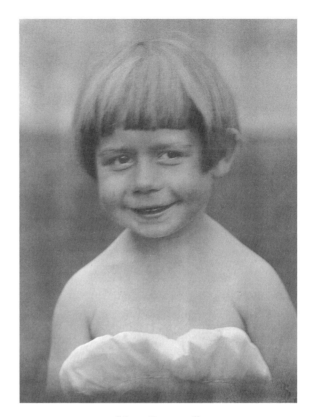

"Just Buttons"

Buttons

One of the major draws for these productions was a little girl called "Buttons," who became a celebrity in Northeast Minneapolis. She was a favorite little star and people from all over the city came to specifically see her unrehearsed candor. The *Star Journal* featured her regularly in stories about the pageants. Some of the headlines read-"Buttons is going to have a prominent part, watch her!"

"Buttons," whose real name was Margaret Moerls, won the hearts of the audience when she was only two and the smallest in a chorus of little girls who sang the "song of the buttons" at a performance of the "Three Bears" and became the hit of the evening. So much so that she won herself the name of "Buttons," which stayed with her throughout her life.

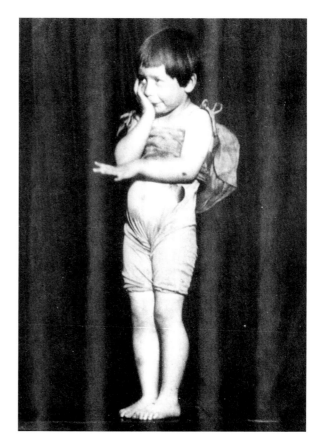

Buttons as cupid in Valentine's Dance summer 1920.

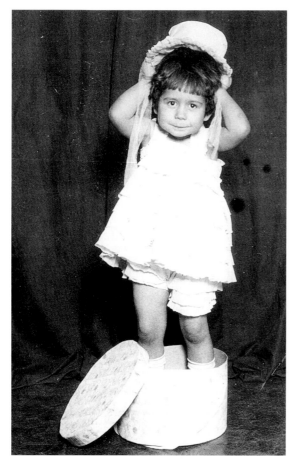

Winter pageant in 1920s called the "French Hat Box Dance" age three.

The next year Margaret Moerls, at age three, played Cupid in a Valentine dance. But she thought she was going to be a little round button again. "Will you be Mrs. Dietz's Cupid and dance with the big girls?" she was asked. Her mouth drooped and she shook her head. The director was puzzled, for Margaret loved to please.

"Yes," but the tears were beginning to fall. "But I don't want to be Cupid. I want to be Mrs. Dietz's button"

Buttons stole the show because she always danced about two steps behind everybody else in the class; her legs were so short that she simply couldn't keep up. But she tried so hard, taking it very seriously, and always with a smile.

Buttons performed in pageants from 1919 to 1922, until she took ill with scarlet fever. She did recover but never danced in the pageants after that.

Costumes

In addition to all of her other duties, Mrs. Dietz took time to help the girls with their costumes, which always caused a great amount of commotion: "Mrs. Dietz, my Mama says "what kind of cloth?" "Mrs. Dietz, my Mama works and she can't make my dress. Can you help me?" "Mrs. Dietz, my big sister says she is sorry but sugar went up again, and we can't buy my goods."

Of course, she had time, and she purchased pink-flowered-fabric for the Old Fashioned Dance, cheesecloth for another. Yes, Mrs. Dietz would find time to cut out several costumes, and constructed them using a sewing machine lent by a neighbor and with the aid of the little dancers themselves. By some magic, material that the home folks could not afford, would find itself in the little dancer's hands.

Hundreds of costumes were completed for each performance. The older girls made their own from the material furnished by the park board, cutting them by the pattern given by the playground instructor so that they would be exactly alike.

And all this time several other activities were going on like sewing, nature classes, basketry, and story telling, with gymnasium in the evenings and boys and girls clubs of every denomination. In the middle of dance rehearsal, a child would come rushing in to say that another butterfly has hatched out, and there was a general rush to see it.

Among the 150 girls 11 nationalities were represented. And the children had to govern themselves peaceably when Mrs. Dietz was called away to fill one of her many parts as director of the fieldhouse and was unable to supervise them.

Mrs. Dietz becomes Park Director

Later Mrs. Dietz became the director of the recreation center for the Board of Park Commissioners and supervised children's pageants all over the city. Every child in Minneapolis could learn a beautiful dance, with the added incentive of appearing in a richly costumed production. "There are only two requirements," said Mrs. Dietz. "The child must have the written consent of their parents and must attend rehearsals regularly. The lessons are of course free and no child is barred from inability to pay for her costume."

The first citywide pageant was presented in 1918 by 300 children from 16 playgrounds and was witnessed by 10,000 spectators. "Mother Goose" was performed and illuminated with kerosene lamps. It was crude in comparison with the electrically lighted finished production of the "Giant and the Pygmy," performed on July 1, 1931, with a cast of 1,200 children from 32 playgrounds and witnessed by approximately 40,000 spectators.

From 1918 to 1930, there were pageants every year. They were performed at such places as Lyndale Park, Lake Harriet Roof Garden, East High School Auditorium, Logan Park, and the American Legion Post in Northeast Minneapolis.

Alice Dietz, known as "park pageanteer extraordinary," retired in 1957. Two hundred and fifty people honored her. Her patience and kindness to all the children who gathered at Logan Park will not be forgotten.

Mrs. Dietz and Buttons 1920.

Community Sings at Windom Park

The contestants at Logan Park Community Sing winning the Minneapolis Daily News Banner 1921.

Windom Park hosted a tradition of "Community Sings" in the 1930s and 1940s. Band concerts and community sings drew large numbers of people during the summer months.

Community sings had been started during World War I by the Minneapolis Park Board to boost morale in the 1920s. *The Minneapolis Tribune* joined in the sponsorship. Community sings lasted until the 1950s throughout Minneapolis.

But nowhere in Minneapolis were such sings greeted with as much enthusiasm as they were in Windom Park. Harry Anderson, a Minneapolis music teacher, was the song leader at Windom Park. During his 25 years of conducting, he led community sings with audiences that included the famous and even royalty. Former president Herbert Hoover listened by radio to one of the park sings. Anderson once went to Winnipeg, Canada, to lead residents in a sing for King

George and Queen Elizabeth of England. The Windom singers were defending champions in the community sing competition that the newspaper sponsored.

A wooden bandshell was originally constructed on the hill just west of the current playground in Windom Park. It burned down in the late 1940s or early 1950s, so a cement band shell was constructed where the park building now stands. The current park building was built in 1964. At one time the park had a well with a pump where visitors could come and have a cool drink.

The old portable bandstand that was transported from park to park for the neighborhood concerts 1907.

Competition in the Parks

In 1930, the *Minneapolis Tribune* introduced the giant "sing" trophy into the competition. The singers were judged on enthusiasm (40 percent), attendance (40 percent), and deportment (20 percent). Leaders in the competition throughout the years were Powderhorn and Fairview parks. Each of them was given the

A crowd at Windom Park reaches for the trophy it won in 1943.

trophy seven times. Windom won it six times. Proof of the popularity of the sings was the attendance. A banner year was 1950 when the sings attracted 90,504 people to 47 sing sessions throughout the city

George Murk, a young Minneapolis baritone, took over the director's job when Anderson died in 1946.

In 1951, Dowley Clark, a former Minneapolis newspaperman, asked to have a recording of a "typical Minneapolis community sing" in a letter he sent to the *Minneapolis Tribune*. He wanted to teach the Greek people community sings patterned after the Minneapolis program.

Old songs remained the most popular at the sings. "Put Your Arms Around Me, Honey," was the leader in 1952. Runners-up were "I Like Mountain Music," and "Take Me Out to the Ball Game." The program also included hymns, current hits, marches, and waltzes.

5 Cemeteries, Gravestones, and Funeral Chapels

Gravestones Tell a Historical Tale

Beltrami Park, the former Maple Hill Cemetery, 1100 Polk Street Northeast, started out as Maple Hill, an 1857 private cemetery, where many Civil War veterans were buried. Kids use to play in the cemetery, playing mumble-peg and Duck on the Rock. They used stones for bases and the mound of a grave for the pitcher's box. One dark night, two youngsters took up all the old stone markers and threw them down the side of a hill. A short time later, the two boys sickened and died. The neighborhood mothers said that was a curse for disturbing the dead, an old Italian belief.

The cemetery was closed in 1891. In 1894, more than 1,000 bodies were moved to Sunset and Hillside cemeteries. In those days the caskets were covered with glass, and as the men were digging, you could hear the tinkle of glass breaking. Bodies were often buried with lots of jewelry. Children watched as the men picked up watches and rings. Eventually, the land was converted to a park and named after Giacomo Beltrami, an Italian explorer who thought he had discovered the source of the Mississippi River in 1823.

Minneapolis Italians presented a monument to honor Beltrami in 1947.

There are still three old marked graves in the park. One is for a woman who died in 1862 at age 30; a second about 100 feet north, was simply marked, "My Husband." The third is for Eldridge M. Tinney, age 47, who died in 1880. The Park Board moved to other cemetaries, the remains of those whose relatives could be located and gave permission. The other graves stayed. In 1973, the Park Board raised the sinking markers and set them in concrete.

At the north end of the park is a granite memorial to the 46 Civil War veterans buried there that reads: "Within the boundaries of this park, which in past days was Maple Hill Cemetery, there rest in the sleep of the ages 46 soldiers of the Grand Army of the Republic. Courageously they responded to our country's call of the war of the rebellion. Gallantly they fought to achieve the victory. Although men's thoughtless actions have deprived them of their right to individually marked and cherished graves, the children of future ages will gather here to honor them." There follows a list of the names of 46 Civil War veterans.

Moving gravestones in Maple Hill Cemetery, now Beltrami Park around 1935.

Funeral Chapels

In 1860, Minneapolis's first undertaker, H.S. Howe, began as a cabinetmaker and upholsterer on the corner of First and Bridge streets. The occupation of furniture maker quite naturally led to producing coffins and from there, to providing services associated with the care of the dead.

The mortuaries of early Minneapolis were unimpressive wooden storefront businesses that often doubled as furniture dealers and looked little different from other commercial buildings. Home reviewals were still common up until World War II, when people began to accept funeral homes as institutions to replace the older funeral customs that were based in the home.

The oldest continuously operated mortuary in Minneapolis that is still in existence is Washburn-McReavy. It began in 1857 and was located at the east end of the original suspension bridge in St. Anthony.

The combined enterprises of furniture and funerals continued in Minneapolis until the 1940s. R. F. Sundseth Furniture and Undertaking; R. F. Bertch; Glessner-Washburn; Burr and Johnson; Billman, Knaeble and Scherer; Kozlak; and Rainville–all operated furniture showrooms as well as funeral services.

The following are brief histories of some of Northeast Minneapolis's funeral chapels.

R. F. BERTCH FUNERAL CHAPEL
1304 University Avenue Northeast

Robert F. Bertch started the first funeral home in lower Northeast in 1905. It had the first motor-driven funeral coach in the Twin Cities. Bertch's first funeral was on April 11, 1906, for a five-year-old girl whose funeral was at St. Boniface Church. Robert's son, Prosper Bertch, and his son-in-law, Walter Theis, later joined him in the business.

Bertch, a German, had two Polish fellows working for him–Stanley Kapala and Charlie Murlowski, two of the most colorful characters in the area. Not your usual idea of somber funeral directors, both were friendly, and fun-loving, with strong personalities. On Saturday night it was a tradition for Stan Kapala, wearing his ever-present derby hat, to put a bunch of roses into a large vase, walk into the 101 Bar, and give each woman a rose. When he left, he would say, "Good night folks, hope to see you soon!"

These two made furniture, and Stanley did beautiful upholstery work. In 1922, the funeral home burned, causing $28,166 in damage. Charlie died very young in 1928.

BILLMAN-HUNT FUNERAL CHAPEL
2701 Central Avenue Northeast

Established in 1908 by Sam Billman and Roy Hunt, the funeral chapel was formerly at 2518 Central Avenue. Billman and Hunt built a new building in 1955 on 2701 Central. It was the first new funeral home after World War II and was also the first one with off-street parking. It is still in the family, owned by John, Richard (second generation), Robert, and Jeffrey Hunt (third generation).

BUCHINGER-GEARHART FUNERAL CHAPEL
2535 Central Avenue Northeast

This was formerly Fox Sullivan Funeral Chapel, which operated from 1938 to 1967.

Bill Buchinger in driveway of Buchinger Funeral Home 1938.

KAPALA-GLODEK FUNERAL HOME
230 Thirteenth Avenue Northeast

In 1932, Stanley Kapala went to undertaking school and then opened up a funeral home of his own at 1007 Main Street, next to the 101 Bar owned by the Sosniewski family. In 1939, Stanley bought a house located on Fifteenth and Adams, which he moved to Thirteenth Avenue and Third Street, and turned it into a funeral home.

Stanley and Kay (Hafey) Kapala 1935.

Stanley's wife, Martha Gable, had died in 1929 before he opened the newer funeral home, but by 1932, he had remarried. On the way home from a funeral in New Richmond, he and his new wife, Kathryn Hafey, were killed when a train hit their car. When their son, Joe, returned from the Marine Corps in 1946, he took over the funeral home after he recuperated from war injuries.

Joe Kapala in his army uniform 1942.

Thomas ("Tommy") Glodek joined the firm in 1953, after graduating from De La Salle High School and St. Thomas College. The name was changed in 1964 to Kapala-Glodek.

KOZLAK-RADULOVICH FUNERAL CHAPEL
1918 University Avenue Northeast

Stanley Kozlak built the building at 1922-28 University Avenue Northeast (which later housed Jax Cafe) for retail furniture and hardware, and, on the ground floor, for the undertaking business. The second floor was a dance hall. There was also living quarters in the building in what is now the south half of the Roundtable Room. Contract price on the building was $15,600. Joseph Kozlak, Sr., and his brothers built a new mortuary building next door at 1918 University Avenue Northeast. When the mortuary was moved from the original building, that space was rented to Jack Dusenka.

Wedding portrait of Stanley Kozlak and Mary Anna Jaros in 1892.

Cadillac Hearse in front of funeral home 1950s.

LARSON-O. E. OSBORNE CHAPEL
2301 Central Avenue Northeast.

O. E. Larson started the business in 1895 in the Provo building at 1911 Central Avenue. It later moved to 2218 Central. The business is currently under the management of Lawrence Osborne, the grandson of O. E. Larson.

RAINVILLE BROTHERS CHAPEL
2301 Central Avenue Northeast

Edward Rainville came to Minneapolis from Quebec, Canada, when he was 19 years old, during the Civil War in the 1860s. His family had immigrated to Canada from France in 1655. Edward Rainville worked his way up as a millwright for a sawmill on the Mississippi. He started a furniture company in 1892 on Nicollet Island. Later, he branched off into the undertaking business and moved over to Bridge Square at Washington and First (now Marquette), down by the Great Northern Depot and Berman Buckskin. In 1912, he and his sons, Noble and Leo, moved the business to 222 East Hennepin, across from Kresge's and Woolworth's department stores, and it became the largest furniture company on the east side. They sold furniture on the first floor and had a funeral chapel on the second floor. In 1981, after a fire in the building, they moved from that location to 2301 Central Avenue Northeast. Edward's grandsons, Richard, Pat, and Edward Rainville now run the funeral chapel.

Edward J., Elie, Edward Sr. and friends standing in front of Rainville Brothers Building 29 Hennepin Avenue on Nicollet Island 1880s.

WASHBURN-MCREAVY FUNERAL CHAPELS
2901 Johnson Street Northeast

William P. Washburn established the company in 1857[3]. At that time, it was located at the end of the original suspension bridge on the east side or St. Anthony at Second and Central (now East Hennepin). It is the oldest funeral establishment in Minnesota. Donald McReavy joined the firm in 1929.

In 1944, it was at 412 Central Avenue and later moved next door to 405 Central. In 1975, it was moved to the building behind the old East Hennepin Cafe at 200 Fifth Street Northeast, and later, back to Second Avenue and Central.

It has always been family owned. Bill Washburn, Sr., and wife, Kay, now run the business with their son, Bill, Jr., and their daughter, Cindy. They now own 12 funeral chapels in Minneapolis and its suburbs. Two are Northeast: one on Twenty-ninth and Johnson Street Northeast and the other on Forty-first and Central Avenue in Columbia Heights.

[3]Not to be confused with William D. Washburn, prominent flour miller and U. S. senator, among other activities.

Marine Corps monument dedicated to brave servicemen and women who have served the people of the U.S. of America 2002.

Cemeteries

HILLSIDE CEMETERY
2600-Nineteenth Avenue Northeast.

Hillside Cemetery, established in 1890, is located on a plot of land called Thwings' Highland additions, known as one of the highest points of the city. Hillside has a war memorial from the Civil War that identifies it as the William Downs Post 68. The legend reads in part that this is a "sacred burial place for our deceased comrades of the war, 1861-65."

Among those of note buried in Hillside are E. C. Dunning, a prominent pioneer of Minneapolis and president of the early park board system. Also buried there is Lewis Duemke, state representative and state senator and a zealous worker for the Northeast section of the city.

Civil War Memorial 2002.

ST. ANTHONY CEMETERY
2700 Central Avenue Northeast

Gravestones in Center Island of cemetery 2002.

This cemetery, established as the Catholic cemetery in 1851, originally was at Fourteenth and Marshall Street Northeast. Father Augustin Ravoux purchased the 15-acre site that was laid out in a symmetrical plan, with several small landscaped circles. Original paths were named after saints. A monument honoring Patrick Judge, a mill worker killed in the Washburn Mill explosion in 1878, is among several in the cemetery.

Blessed Virgin Mary 2002.

SUNSET MEMORIAL CEMETERY
Twenty-second and St. Anthony Boulevard Northeast

Established in 1927, Sunset has no large monuments, only markers with small headstones level with the ground. The cemetery is laid out in 15 artistically shaped sections, each one containing a central monument. These are the Temple of Love; the International Order of Odd Fellows (IOOF) Monolith, which represents friendship, love, and truth; the Balustrade; the Shrine of the Apostles; the Sermon in Stone; the miniature amphitheater, and the sundial in Sylvan Retreat.

The main monument is the Tower of Memories at the main gate, a masterpiece of Minnesota granite, which rises 75 feet and is illuminated in amber floodlights.

Within its summit rests the beautiful 25-tone set of chimes, one of the world's finest carillon towers.

There is also a sunken pool at the front of the chapel.

Notre Dame de Lourdes School classroom early 1900s.

6 Parochial Schools

Parochial schools were an important part of the life of many Roman Catholic and Lutheran families in Northeast Minneapolis. Although there are fewer such schools today than there were, they provided the foundation for thousands of young people over the years. These schools were usually from grade one through eighth grade. From there, the students either were introduced to the public high schools or went to a Catholic high school.

The first Roman Catholic Church in Minneapolis, St. Anthony of Padua, was built in 1849, in what was then called St. Anthony. Four years later, in 1853, a parish school was opened in a rented store. The sisters of St. Joseph were the teachers. By 1866, the church was able to build a schoolhouse. In 1875, a school was opened at St. Boniface parish at 629 Second Street Northeast.

As the city developed, new parishes were established and new schools opened. In 1956, the city had 32 parish schools with a total enrollment of 15,528 pupils. These schools were staffed by sisters from eight different religious communities: St. Anthony, St. Boniface, Holy Cross, St. Cyril, St. Hedwig, All Saints, Our Lady of Lourdes, and De La Salle.

St. Anthony's parish school extended instruction beyond the elementary grades and established a secondary school with 350 girls enrolled. Four Catholic high schools had a total of 2,671 students in 1956. They were taught by 79 teachers in religious orders and 44 lay teachers.

In 1969, a momentous decision was made to close all the schools in the Northeast area with the exceptions of St. Boniface, St. Cyril, and Holy Cross, and merge all of the schools into those three. The name Northeast Regional Catholic School was given to the consolidated school system. St. Cyril contained kindergarten through third grade and most of its faculty were lay persons; the few remaining sisters were no longer exclusively the School Sisters of Notre Dame, but also the Sisters of St. Francis of Assisi from Sylvania, Ohio.

After a few years of declining enrollment, St. Boniface School closed, and in 1986, St. Cyril School followed suit for the same reason. Northeast Catholic Regional School at Holy Cross remains strong with an enrollment of 180.

William S. King residence at 41 Island Avenue on Nicollet Island in 1910. Early Christian Brothers Residence

DE LA SALLE HIGH SCHOOL
One De La Salle Drive (Nicollet Island)

De La Salle High School is one of the Lasallian schools in the country named for Jean Baptiste de La Salle, a French priest who lived in the seventeenth century and devoted his life to building Catholic schools for children of all economic classes. There are 79 La Sallian schools throughout the world. He also founded a religious order of teachers called the Christian Brothers.

After the Christian Brothers started a successful school in St. Paul in 1889, Brother Gideon and Brother Lewis arrived in Minneapolis to open a school. They opened the school in an old orphanage at Sixth Avenue North and Third Street, but the building was not suitable for school purposes. Financial reasons made it impossible to build, so the Brothers withdrew in 1891. When Anthony Kelly died and left $10,000 for a school, Archbishop John Ireland and Archbishop John J. Keane took up a cooperative cause to use this money for the building of a school.

Ground was purchased on Nicollet Island and the building was erected in the spring of 1900. This was a vocational school called Hennepin Institute. The first graduating class of 13 received their diplomas in June of 1903. Brother Heraclian, the second director of De La Salle, wrote letters to many businesses in the area and secured jobs for all 13 graduates.

Early Growth

The school quickly outgrew the original building and an addition was put on in 1907. The enrollment for 1914 was 352 pupils. In 1920, De La Salle switched from a vocational school to a college preparatory four-year high school. The "B" building was erected in 1922 after the rest of the William S. King Estate on Nicollet Island was purchased. In the 1930s, De La Salle continued to prosper and developed a statewide reputation for superior education of young men.

The year 1931 was probably one of the greatest in the history of De La Salle athletics. Led by Coach George Roberts, the basketball team became National Catholic High School Champions. The athletic director was Brother Eugene.

World War II and Postwar Changes

During World War II, the De La Salle student body responded to the spirit of the times and spent much of their non-class time in support of the war effort. Some of the activities included a Victory War Bond Campaign, the donation of blood by students and faculty, scrap drives, first-aid classes, and the introduction of an accelerated graduation program for seniors of draft age. Courses were provided in aeronautics, navigation, and telegraphy for those students who were interested.

In the summer of 1950, the Christian Brothers moved into their new residence at the back of the main school building. It is now used as the Admissions Building and 12 Brothers from the teaching and support staff still live on the upper floors, having abandoned the old King mansion that had been constructed before the American Civil War.

After the war, the student body doubled, reaching over 800 by 1952. A statue of St. John Baptiste De La

A view of Minneapolis and Nicollet Island in 1878 from the roof of the Winslow House.

Salle was presented to the school by the classes of 1951 and 1952, and placed in the courtyard. Because the school could not house all of its students, a public school building in south Minneapolis was acquired. It was known as the Wentworth Building. By 1954, the enrollment exceeded 1,000.

During the 1950s, De La Salle was the only Catholic boys' school in the city. It maintained a prominent position in the state's high school athletic competitions. From 1954 through 1957 and again in 1959, the basketball team won the State Catholic Championships under the direction of Coach Dick Reinhart. Bill Johnson was basketball coach at the Wentworth Building and assisted Coach Reinhart.

To keep up with enrollment, a new addition known as the "A" building was constructed in 1959. The Wentworth building was then closed and the freshmen moved onto Nicollet Island with the upperclassmen.

Enrollment Peaks and Other Changes

During the 1960s, enrollment peaked, reaching 1,651 students by 1964. And at the close of the decade, it had dropped down to 1,000. An increase of Catholic high schools in the area and a decrease in Catholic boys of high school age were thought to be the cause.

In the 1960s, the first woman teacher was hired. This was quite an event for the 60-year-old school. In 1969, the school hired its first lay director, Robert Casanova. Curriculum variations and innovative programs were introduced to make students more personally responsible for their studies. These transformations were going on throughout the nation. De La Salle adopted the "Model Schools" program, which was a radical departure from traditional academics. It proved to be inappropriate and was abandoned in the early 1970s.

On February 28, 1971, Building "C," the oldest of the school's buildings, burned down. St. Anthony of Padua Girls' School closed, and in the fall of the same year, De La Salle for the first time in its history became a co-educational high school. The class of 1971 was the last class of all boys. Other high schools did the same. By 1975, the enrollment had fallen to 480, the lowest level since 1935.

There was serious concern that De La Salle, like other Twin Cities Catholic schools, might be one of the schools to close its doors. But due to the great efforts of the school principals during this period, Brother Litecky and Brother Rothweiler, 10,000 alumni and long-time friends of the school contributed generously to meet the operating costs that were not covered by student tuitions.

Enrollment was down in 1990, but up in 2000. Students do not have to be Catholic to attend, but religious studies are required all four years, and students and teachers pray before each class and before assembly. The school attributes its success in capital campaigns to its large group of loyal alumni. De La Salle celebrated its centennial on May 6 and May 7, 2000.

De La Salle won the National Basketball Championship in 1931.

ALL SAINTS CATHOLIC GRADE SCHOOL
428 Northeast Fifth Street

First Communion Day at All Saints.

On October 30, 1917, ground was broken for the new combined building that would house All Saints Catholic Church and School. On September 3, 1918, the school opened for the first time under the supervision of sisters of St. Francis of Sylvania, Ohio. Faculty sisters were Sisters M. Evangelist, M. Salome, M. Judith, M. Wilfreda, M. Ethelreda, M. Francesca, and M. Jolenta.

The first school commencement was on June 18, 1919. The first graduates were Francis J. Narog, Edward Gable, Anna Micek, Helen Fudali, Mary Mruz, Mary Julkowski, Mary Witkowski, and Mary Kurpiesz. The first crowning of the Blessed Virgin Mary school procession took place in May, 1919. Anna Micek and Sister Mary Agnes were chosen to represent the school children for the crowning. This procession became an annual event. That same year, on May 3, with the May crowning, the Millenium of Christianity in Poland was observed.

An essay contest was held for all parochial schools in the St. Paul Diocese on December 5, 1920. Two students at All Saints School were awarded prizes: Eighth grader Andrew Holewa won a first prize, and sixth grader John Fudali won a first prize.

On June 15, 1923, a storm cloud burst and the school was flooded with three feet of water in the building. Men from the church worked till 3:00 a.m. Sunday morning to clean up the mess.

In 1939, ground was broken for a new church and school but there were labor problems in building the new school.

In 1976, the church council voted to repair the school rather than build a new one. The school was stuccoed and new windows and doors installed. On November 27, 1977, flood waters struck again: vandals pulled the water sink off the kitchen wall and flooded the entire school building. This was a sad Sunday. Six parishioners mopped and drained for hours, but in vain. The floors buckled and the walls and ceilings cracked. However, fast work on the part of the "Flood Fighters" saved the building from electrical wires shorting out and resulting in fire, but the building had to be repaired again.

All Saints Grade School class of 1961.

Steve Pelewa, the caretaker of the school, was better known as "The Guardian Angel of All Saints School." In the 1970s, All Saints School was closed and the students attended the Regional school, a consolidation of most of the Catholic parochial schools in the area.

Holy Cross Grade School built in 1906.

HOLY CROSS CATHOLIC GRADE SCHOOL
1630 Northeast Fourth Street

In 1888, the first Holy Cross School opened in a small house, which had been moved behind Holy Cross Church on Seventeenth and Fourth Street. The house had four rooms, two of which were converted into classrooms. The classrooms had a large pot-bellied stove in the center and double rows of chairs on both sides. Boys sat on one side and girls on the other. About 40 pupils attended that first year. Three different lay teachers, named Galuszczynski, Kurek, and Kwilinski, taught the pupils successively. When Kwilinski departed, the school was closed and did not reopen until 1894.

New Immigrants Result in School Reopening

More people were arriving from Poland, settling in Northeast Minneapolis, and building homes, so the need for reopening the school became evident. A new church was built in 1892, and the old church was converted into a school. It was divided into two sections with a movable wall, one end for the younger students and the other for the older.

It was hard to get teachers at first. But in 1894, three Franciscan Sisters came to the school. Sister Assumpta, the principal, taught the older children, and Sister Cleopha taught the younger children; Sister Isidore took on the responsibilities of convent housekeeper.

Shortly after the school opened, the first pastor of Holy Cross, Father Pacholski was transferred to another parish. In 1900, the parish bought five lots on Seventeenth Avenue and Fourth Street across the street from the church for $1,800. The land was to be used as a site for a new school and convent. Because of the influx of so many children, a new school building was completed in 1906 at a cost of $50,000. The school was modeled after the St. Boniface School building. Bazaars, picnics at Lake Johanna, and ice cream socials were used to raise money for the school, which had eight classrooms, two large meeting rooms, a library, and a gymnasium-auditorium.

Holy Cross 8th grade graduation in 1926. Back row-Ann Podgorska, Stephanie Lopata, Dorothy Kaczmarek, Wanda Wisniewska, Evelyn Mierocha. Middle row-Augusta Doroba, Margaret Smith, Louise Cieluszak, Helen Tomczyk, Rose Boryczka, Della Ruck. Front row-Emilia Kapala, Valeria Barkiewicz, Frances Sledz, Florence Sledz, Florence Bierch, Mary Sutor, Malinowski, Stella Duda.

A Flourishing School

Holy Cross School continued to flourish with a faculty of 16 sisters. In 1917, the Franciscan Sisters of Sylvania, Ohio, with Sister Leocadia as principal and superior, took charge of the school. Thirty-three girls from Holy Cross became sisters from 1910 to 1927, and several boys joined the priesthood. On April 30, 1950, a new school was dedicated, and in 1953, the recreation center was dedicated. An auditorium-gym and bowling alley consisting of 12 lanes were the main facilities of the recreation center. Chester Mady was the first bowling alley manager and was succeeded by Mel Schroeder. Interest in bowling ran high. In 1983 this space was converted into what is known as the St. Maximilian Kolbe Center, which is used for funeral luncheons and meeting room for bingo and socializing events.

Athletics played an important role in the history of the school and parish. Many of the young men went on to play on great high school teams and on college teams in the area. Some of the teams Holy Cross played against were Resurrection, St. Anne's, Boys Home, St. Charles, Incarnation, St. Lawrence, St. Anthony, St. Helena, Notre Dame, Annunciation, Ascension, St. Stephens, and Holy Rosary. School championships were taken in the following years: 1922, baseball; 1927, state basketball; 1949, basketball; and 1947, softball. School plays, musicals, and Dramatic Club activities were very important and loved activities for the kids.

Dramatic Club Production "Cheaper by the Dozen" 1950. Joe Godava, Mary Ann Miekoday, Frank Burmis, Donald Lubinski, Sylvia Schutta, Dale Jorgensen, Lorraine Partyka, Joe Dircz, Mary Ann Walker, Veronica Kocon and Clellmont.

Decline and Consolidation

During the 1960s, church collections and school enrollment declined significantly. A 1970 census showed there were only 2,915 members in the parish with 474 children under the age of 12. This decline, which was happening all around the city, made it necessary to consolidate the Northeast parish schools. Eleven parishes joined to form the Northeast Regional School System of Parochial Schools. Each parish subsidized the system with an amount according to the number of students it sent. At first, the buildings of Holy Cross, St. Cyril, and St. Boniface were used and rent was paid for the use of the buildings. Later St. Cyril and St. Boniface were closed.

8th grade graduation 1919.

Holy Cross Cheerleaders 1949. Front row-Donna Wojciak, Rose Lewandowski, Anita Maslowski, Lorraine Basara. Back row-Fr. Ted Koziol, Noel Grech, Betty Kohler, Betty Blahut, Marilyn Birnstiel, Lorraine Partyka.

1927 State Basketball Champions. Front row-Frank Kostick, Mike Cieluszak, Mike Britt, Chuck Samek, Roman Majeski. Top row-Frank Pelak, Stan Kasmer, Al Kreszowski, Fr. Ceiminski, Frank Worwa, Zig Bishop.

1922 Parochial Baseball Champions. Front row-Joseph Kowalczyk, Leo Hawloski, Walter Weiss, Ralph Rucki, Walter Krawczyk. Middle row-Al Kreszowski, Joseph Tomaszewski, Henry Meka, Ed Rucki, Julian Boryczka. Top row-Fr. Vincent Worzalla, Stanley Wojciak, Joseph Stanek, Raymond Stawski, Fred Wines, Edward Dombeck, Frank Kozlak, Louis Jaros, Fr. Joseph Cieminski.

Notre Dame Parochial School 1934.

OUR LADY OF LOURDES CATHOLIC GRADE SCHOOL
605 Northeast Fifth Street

Notre Dame de Lourdes had its beginning in 1855 at St. Anthony of Padua Church which once had a French emphasis. The first Our Lady of Lourdes School opened in 1885 in the church basement. In 1888, a new school building was constructed in the midst of the Canadian settlement. The Grey Nuns of Montreal supplied all of the teachers. The nuns taught Latin, music and English. Father Dennis Ledon taught French. Although it was a Catholic School, anyone who came could be dismissed from religion classes.

At that time in French Canada and some other provinces and countries, Roman Catholicism and government were merged; the churches were paid by the state and by household taxes. In the United States, the church and state are separate, so it was difficult to set up a Catholic school system. In the 1890 school year, the Grey Nuns taught 128 people ages 13 to 22, during after school hours. During the pastorate of Father John Andre in 1901, the parish had reached its fulfillment with a completed church, school, and convent. At that time, 290 children were in the parochial school.

In 1906 the Grey Nuns withdrew and the Sisters of St. Joseph took charge. In 1910, the school began teaching English instead of French. The new pastor wanted to rebuild the school in 1924, which would cost $80,000, and bring it closer to the church. If it couldn't be done, he wanted to move the church. The parishioners and parents were not happy with this, and he left. The school enrollment was 206 in 1927.

In 1934 Sisters Edwina, Adolpha, Sylvania, Louise Joseph and Marie Aubert taught 181 students. In 1944 Sisters Marie Arthur, Josephine, Leone, Rufina and Agnese taught 135 students. In 1953 Sisters M. Lucienne, Rose Margaret, Antoinette and St. Gregory taught 126 students.

Students walked from the school to the church for services. They'd parade down the Northeast streets by classes. They didn't have school and church on the same block like other parochial schools.

There was an annual paper sale where the furnace room would be piled with papers. The lunchroom had a bench around the outside walls, and a few tables. The older students used the tables and the younger ones used benches. Although the school didn't serve food, the students brought their lunches from home.

During World War II, heating the school was really a problem because fuel oil was rationed. Enrollment was down and very few who were enrolled belonged to the parish. Several other Catholic schools were within a few blocks. The number of sisters was cut down from four to three in 1957. The school was closed, and the last class graduated in the spring of 1959. The school was sold to the Minneapolis Housing and Redevelopment Authority for $19,000 and the building was razed in 1960.

Noble and Josephine Rainville would take the Sisters of St. Joseph out for a picnic in the countryside in the late 1930s. Sisters Edwina, Louise Joseph, Emelita, Ignace, Bertha, Adolpha, Antoinette, Mary Grace and Leontine.

Memories of Our Lady of Lourdes School in the 1920s

By Corinne Diffley

I remember walking to school in dresses and long black stockings that Grandma knitted. They were woolen in the winter and cotton in the summer. On our feet we wore deer hide moccasins. We had art only once a month and even the poorest kids took music lessons, either piano or violin for 50 cents each. The recitals were held in the parlor, which had one light in the center and was filled with beautiful Boston ferns.

There were Lebanese, Irish, and Italian kids who came to the school. Some lived in the old Flats that were right next-door on Washington Street. They all had to learn French and often they could pronounce the words better than the French Canadian kids.

It was fun to walk down and watch the lamplighter who would go around with a stick and light the gas streetlights about 5:00 in the evening. There was one on each corner.

My brother, George Belair remembers that the furnace burned coal and wood and needed to be cleaned frequently. The ashes were dumped on the school playground, and the kids played "king of the hill" on the filthy mounds, much to the Sisters' dismay.

We had an All Class Reunion on September 5th, 1992. A Mass was held at 3:00 at Our Lady of Lourdes Church. Then we had a social hour followed by a special dinner at Jax Café at 6:00 P.M. 230 people attended from twelve different states including the Yukon Territory, California, Arizona, Maryland, Washington, New Mexico, Florida, Texas and Indiana. It was one of the first of its kind in the nation, an "All Class Reunion" for an elementary school.

Harmonica Band 1934. Back row-Madeline Rivet, Dorothy Skenlon, Bertha Paquette, Mary Cyr, Middle row-Phyllis Gagnon, Patricia Dargis, Phyllis Paquette, Jane Raymond, Annabelle Hurley. Front row-Gerald Paquette, Richard Martinson, Willard Murphy, Eugene Belair, Robert Paquette, Ronald Raymond.

Notre Dame de Lourdes first and second grade class of 1922.

Notre Dame de Lourdes class of 1935. Back row-Arley Lapointe, Maurice Morneau, Irene Lambert, Rosemary Smith, Lorraine Coulombe, Elaine Poisson, Yvonne Durand, Alice Rouselle, Eva Bochet, Robert Schwachtgen, Thomas Gagne. Front row-Louis Rivet, Charles Archambualt, Mary Fitzpatrick, Audre L Herault, Elaine Paquette, Catherine Anton, Lucille Beaubien, Juliette Murphy, Lorraine Poisson, Bernard Coulombe, Laurence Smith, Father Bazin.

St. Anthony of Padua Senior Sleigh Ride at Hilltop Riding Academy with Christmas party following afterwards on December 22, 1946. Bottom row-Patricia Kelvie, Mary Gallagher, Lois Spanjers, Gail Griffin, Evelyn Hanson, Jeanne Peters, Shirley Coffey, Jeanne Talbot, Harriet Manthey, Phyllis Green, Marjorie Runcie. Second row-Jeanne Kuppe, Mary Green, Genevieve Gauthier, Patricia Doherty, Leone Shields, Margaret Cavanagh, Ruth Freund, Kathleen Egan, Patricia Demuelles, Lois Gilbert, Virginia DesLauriers, Mary Fjeran. Third row-Beverly Harvey, Jeanne Morneau, Geraldine Soltys, Rosemary Micek, Kathleen Foley, Pauline Johnson, Mary Wallen, Kathleen Paquette, Donna Hyser, Phyllis McGowan. Fourth row-Betty Hargarten, Amarylyss Bretschneider, Betty Shelley, Patricia Barry, Eileen Ritter, Juanita Welle, Patricia Graca, Marie Altman, Dorothy Zelenak, Anne Rabatin, Margaret Kovalik, Mary Louise Mangen, Dorothy McLaughlin, Blanche Klein, Ida Ferrian, Lois Bell, Patricia Kane.

ST. ANTHONY OF PADUA GRADE SCHOOL AND HIGH SCHOOL
804 Second Street Northeast

St. Anthony of Padua High School 1946.

In 1853, two nuns came from St. Paul to open a school in a vacant fur-trading store in the town of St. Anthony. Reverend Denis Ledon, pastor of St. Anthony of Padua Parish, had called the nuns, Sister Philomene and Sister Ursula, who established the convent and school in 1853. When Father Ledon was called to the St. Paul Cathedral, the school closed in January of 1860, and the nuns went back to St. Paul. But the following year they returned and reopened the school.

This early school was a large two-and-a-half story frame building that had ten rooms, five on each floor. On the first floor was one classroom for the girls and another for the boys, a music room, a parlor, and a kitchen. It was able to accommodate 30 boarders and 80 scholars. At that time, the attendance varied from 40 to 50 pupils.

In 1867, during Father Tissot's pastorate, a new brownstone school was built on the east side to accommodate the ever-increasing number of pupils. The building fronted Second Street and contained four large classrooms. At this time, a high school department was added to the parish school, and the private school, which had been maintained in the Convent by the Sisters from their first coming, had closed. The pupils who had been attending it were transferred to the new parish school building. The first high school graduating class of 1885 had three members: Annie Bohan (Walsh), Dolly Fleetham (Hoy), and Mary Jarret (Sister Josepha).

Growth

For 20 years, the old stone structure, with its Gothic windows and the new brick building fronting Second Street, was sufficient. But in 1910, Father Patrick Kenny realized the two buildings were no longer adequate. He undertook the task of erecting a new building, which contained 15 rooms devoted to class work. On the main floor was a gymnasium and large auditorium.

The St. Anthony "Female Academy" in 1933 was located where the convent building now stands except that it faced Eighth Avenue. The school had two rooms; Sister Frances was the teacher. Lessons began promptly at 9 a.m. Studies consisted of catechism, grammar, spelling, history, geography, writing, and Bible history. There was no lighting system, and when it was dark they used candles at first, and later kerosene lamps.

Grand march at Junior-Senior Prom held at the old Radisson Hotel in downtown Minneapolis April 11, 1945.

Scout Troup #54-organized in 1939 First row-James Midlo, James McGowan, Thomas Strand, Gerald Miller, Eugene Lambert, Thomas Thies. Middle row-Thomas Martinson, Wallace John, Thomas Schneider, Rodney Biedron, James Lappen. Third row-Reverend R.J. Moorman, Earl Huber, Lauren Begin, John Loyas, Gary Cochran, Walter Traczyk.

In 1960, a new structure was built with a two-story grade school wing with eight classrooms and a gymnasium. A three-story high school wing housed a library, chemistry and biology lab, administration offices, and faculty rooms. The elementary section had space for 300 children, and the high school accommodated 400 girls. The addition was built for $350,000. The new construction separated grade and high school departments that had been in one building since 1910.

Closing the School

St. Anthony of Padua School closed and was torn down in 1982 to make way for St. Anthony Eldercare. Because the school had meant so much to so many people, a large crowd came out to attend a special service that was held to honor and say goodbye to the 129-year-old school. The service began in the church with song, prayer, and brief remarks. A procession through the school ended in the gym of the 1959 addition, which was designated to be the future dining and activities center for Catholic Eldercare. Refreshments were served and friendships were renewed as former students exchanged memories. The Sisters of St. Joseph, who staffed the school, were there to greet former students.

Eighth Grade graduates 1949 First row-James Midlo, James Lappen, Richard Johnson, Kenneth Hartley, John Crawley, Eugene Lambert. Second row-Joan Raleigh, Josephine Sevanich, Carol Polsek, Mertice Rehdahl, Gail Wall, Thomas Strand. Third row-Thomas Thies, Thomas Schneider, Elaine Rucinski, Cecilia Menard, Antoinette Hanson, Patrick Irving, James McGowan. Fourth row-Joseph Conly, Joseph Hershfield, Lauren Begin, John Loyas, Gary Cochran, Raymond Malark, Earl Huber, Rodney Biedron.

Thoughts of my years at St. Anthony High School

By Alice Rainville

Donna Gates, Ardis Weisner, Lois Melsha, and Bernie Sentyrz on the night of Gay 90 Review in 1945.

Our class of 1946 had 80 girls, which was considered a large number. There were about 300 to 400 in the entire school. Young women who came from parochial grade schools all across Minneapolis attended St. Anthony of Padua High School. It was not unusual for families to send 4-6 girls to St. Anthony for high school and their sons to De La Salle. From north Minneapolis, my three sisters and I attended St. Anthony and my brother Patrick, De La Salle. Tuition for fall of 1942 was $40.00 or $4.00 per month plus fees and books. That seemed like a lot of money!

The "Second Street Flyer" stopped at the front door of our school. A smaller streetcar on Broadway and the Lowry bus were our east-west links. In my four years from 1942 to 1946, gas rationing and the Second World War shortages made good shoes and good transit critical. Tokens were 6 for 45 cents and transfers were free.

Uniforms were navy blue wool serge jumpers, Princess style of modest length, which was just below the knee, with white long sleeve blouses. Many of the jumpers were homemade. Long stockings, nylons or bobby socks were worn with gray oxford shoes, a navy blue cardigan sweater and navy blue "Beanie" as appropriate head wear for church services.

Sister Anselm directed special events. We had a strong active Glee Club accompanied by Catherine Wolfe, who was from the Basilica of St. Mary Parish. One or two plays or operettas were performed annually. If we needed males, De La Salle guys were invited to try out. Our school paper was titled the "Anthonian."

Our Girls Club of ten was formed late in my sophomore year. The club is named "Entre Nous" which means "Between Us or Among Us." Naming the club was my contribution reflecting two years of French study while others took Latin. Our friendships have been constant over the years and enriched by our appreciation to the Sisters of St. Joseph of Carondolet and the host parish, St. Anthony of Padua. One of our club members has died and we miss her. We celebrated our 50th class reunion at the Nicollet Island Inn in 1996.

Alice Rainville on her graduation day taken in front of her family's house in 1946.

Senior Year Dance at Minneapolis Auto Club (Triple A), a very prestigious place 1946.

St. Boniface Catholic Grade School in the 1950s, built in 1927 and torn down in 1970.

ST. BONIFACE CATHOLIC GRADE SCHOOL
640 University Avenue Northeast

The first school building for St. Boniface was erected on Seventh Avenue and Main Street in 1868. Made from stone quarried on the site, it was a one-story, two-room structure. Mr. Ruff, Peter Thielen, and Joseph Ingenhutt taught the classes. The tuition was 75 cents a year. Forty students were enrolled.

When the new frame church was erected on Seventh and Second Street, the lumber salvaged from the old church was used to build the sisters' house and the school. The Sisters of Christian Charity of the Immaculate Heart of Mary took over the teaching in 1875. There were four sisters: Sister Cornelia, Sister Conradine, Sister Paula, and Sister Symphorosa. In 1883, the second floor was added. In 1894, 220 children attended the school. The Young Ladies' Sodality was started in 1893.

The existing school was small and in constant need of repair. In 1903, a new school was built on Seventh Avenue and University. The eight classrooms occupied the first floor, while a hall and stage were on the second floor. The old school was sold for $600.

In 1915, property was bought south of the school to be used as a playground for the children. In 1932, John Torberg, who had taught grade school, became organist and music teacher. In 1950, the basement was remodeled for use as a kindergarten. In 1958, Philip Wagner took over teaching the upper grade boys. Three bowling alleys were in the basement of the old church and they were in use all the time.

Play at St. Boniface 1950s.

Eighth grade graduating class of 1930.

Memories of St. Boniface School in the 1920s

By Margaret Hoben

We had German class every day. On Friday afternoons the girls had embroidery class. By the time we got to the 4th grade we graduated to pillowcases. The boys had drawing during this time. We also went to church every day and were expected to attend the 8:30 Children's Mass on Sunday and Benediction at 3:00 on Sunday afternoons. No excuses. If any of the kids were naughty they would have to go to sit in the cloakroom. Once there were 2 girls who came to school after they had gotten their hair cut in a bob. They had to sit in the cloakroom for a week. Then when they came back to class, they had to wear a hat.

There was a tunnel that went from the church basement to the school. But you would have to go through the furnace room that was really spooky. The boys would always try to scare us. There was also a bowling alley in the school basement. The 7th and 8th graders were separated. The girls were in the first classroom in the front of the building and were taught by the nuns. The boys were taught by our organist, Mr. Torberg in the back classroom. The only class they had together was music.

We had an All School Reunion on September 30, 2001. Three hundred seventy-five people attended. Three of our nuns attended. Two were from Chicago and one from New Orleans. We had a Mass with a special Alumni Choir. Later there was a social hour and a program given by Father Vincent and a dinner served in the church hall.

St. Boniface graduating class of 1957.

Kindergarten class at St. Charles 1951.

ST. CHARLES BORROMEO CATHOLIC GRADE SCHOOL

2727 Northeast Stinson Boulevard

The St. Charles Borromeo School opened in September of 1939 with over 180 students enrolled in K-8. The Sisters of St. Joseph of Carondelet, led by Sister Grata, the principal and Mother of the convent staffed the school. The first teachers included Sisters Carlotta, St. Ireneus, Leone, Marie Edward, Ethel, St. Bridget, Anna Mary, Andrina, and St. Claire. Mary Landy taught dramatic art classes. Tuition for the school year was $1 for the first child in a family, and 75 cents for any additional children.

In 1951, Sister Mary Magdalene, the school principal, was confronted with a serious overcrowding problem after enrollment had mushroomed from 498 to 650 students in only three years. In that same year, two wings were added to the church-school building, providing 12 additional classrooms, a new library, and a cafeteria with separate dining for boys and girls.

Graduating class of 1941 St. Charles Borromeo.

Growth and New Buildings

In 1957, six lay teachers were added to the faculty of four sisters to teach 992 students. To help offset expenses, tuition was increased by $5 per child to $25. The following year, kindergarten classes were discontinued because of school overcrowding.

When the new church was built in 1959, the old one was made into a gymnasium. The population in St. Anthony Village and in Northeast Minneapolis swelled in 1960. For the first time in the school's history, enrollment surpassed 1,000 students in eight grades. Sister Rose Carmel succeeded Sister Gabriel as school principal.

Throughout the 1960s and 1970s, the number of sisters teaching in the school had steadily declined. In 1974, the five remaining Sisters of St. Joseph of Carondelet completed the order's last year at St. Charles, which had served for 35 years. Father Spack, Christine Lore, and Mary Lyons, the first lay teacher in the school, who had taught for 23 years, also left.

Father George Freeman and four sisters from the Order of St. Francis joined the staff. But they were not directly associated with the school. Spiraling inflation combined with a recession and the loss of educational tax credits placed a severe financial crunch on the parish. The finance committee worked to develop a plan to maintain a viable school program, and parishioners were encouraged to make financial sacrifices

Enrollment in the school stabilized in the mid-1970s after a decade of declining enrollment. The 500 students attending in 1975 were taught by a dedicated staff of 19 lay teachers. An unprecedented number of students from St. Charles-Joe Debbins, Diane Geisel, Lisa Juricko, and Betsy Opland-were selected to participate in the Minnesota State Science Fair competition. The national energy crisis during this time affected St. Charles, and the Day School was closed on Mondays for several weeks to save fuel.

Principal Gary Wilmer and students at St. Charles Borromeo 1988.

During the late 1970s, the 40-year-old school building was updated with a modern kitchen, a large meeting room, and a girls' locker room. An endowment for the school was formed to offset the increasing cost of Catholic education. In 1980, Helen Peterson retired after 25 years of teaching at the parish school. In 1985, the National Catholic Education Association selected Gary Wilmer as "the Principal of the Year."

After 16 years of outstanding service to the parish as assistant principal, teacher, and coach, Craig Vana left St. Charles to become principal at another school in 1985. In 1988, Sister Rosaria left after six years of dedicated service. Two new members joined the staff: Sister M. Constantia and Christopher Ruff, a lay theologian.

Girls basketball team of St. Charles Borromeo 1980s.

Athletic Superiority

In the fall of 1940, Father Wambach organized a basketball team to play in the City Catholic Boys League. Jim Pearo was coach. Father Wambach appeared to be developing a basketball dynasty at St. Charles; the team won city championships in 1944, 1945, and 1946. In 1953 and 1967, St. Charles celebrated championships in basketball and baseball. The athletic program led by Craig Vana earned a widespread reputation in the 1970s as one of the outstanding parochial school programs. In 1980, the eighth-grade basketball team-the "Green Machine"-defeated St. Mark's of St. Paul 38-37 and posted the best record (30-0) in the school's history. The team also took the championship in 1987. The varsity football team was crowned Twin City champions from 1983 to 1986.

In 1955, the eighth grade girl's basketball team, coached by John Sullivan, captured the school's first girl's city championship. In 1976, 1981, 1982 and 1984 they also won the championship. The girls' softball team won the Minneapolis championship in 1987.

A tornado hit the Twin Cities in 1984 and a great deal of the damage was centered in Northeast Minneapolis. Fortunately, the school building received minor damage, which was a surprise and a blessing since the tornado actually touched down at the corner of Twenty-seventh and Stinson Boulevard.

Many parochial schools throughout the Twin Cities have closed, but St. Charles Borromeo School is still going strong. Gary Wilmer is the principal. The school has an enrollment of 370 in grades K-8. Numerous students are children of former students.

The former receptionist, Mrs. Audrey Puchtel, worked in the school office for 23 years. Audrey was a member of the first eighth grade graduating class of St. Charles. Her children also attended St. Charles. Audrey was an active member of the community and touched many lives there. Unfortunately she died a few years ago, a victim of cancer. Her funeral was the largest ever celebrated at the Church of St. Charles Borromeo.

ST. CYRIL'S CATHOLIC GRADE SCHOOL
1305 Northeast Second Street

Slovak Play at St. Cyril's in 1940.

The third major construction project of the parish was the building of the St. Cyril's parish school. Although the parish began raising funds in 1926, construction was halted by the most severe depression in the nation's history. Actual construction was delayed until 1936, and the school was opened in 1937 under

A group of children attending Reverend Francis Hrachovsky's class of religious instruction 1905.

1938 graduates of St. Cyril's.

St. Cyril's basketball team 1937-38.

the guidance of the School Sisters of Notre Dame. This was done under the leadership of Father Dargay.

The school opened with 127 pupils gathered from 15 different schools. In September of 1939, the ninth grade, with 12 pupils was added. The total enrollment rose to 141 in 1941. In the late 1960s, the school was transferred from parish support and control to a regional one. The school closed in 1986.

ST. HEDWIG'S CATHOLIC GRADE SCHOOL

2919 Northeast Randolph Street

In the beginning, the Sisters of St. Francis from Holy Cross commuted weekly to the small frame church of St. Hedwig's to give catechism instruction. But in 1920, with the erection of the permanent church-school building, it became possible for the parish to realize the hope of a sound Catholic education for its children as a foundation of spiritual growth. An elementary school was organized with the help of the Holy Cross sisters. Sister Estella assisted by Sister Ethelreda and Sister Gertrude came from Sylvania, Ohio, to become the teachers in the new St. Hedwig's school. A parish convent was erected in 1925. In 1964, the school had five sisters and 118 pupils. Some of the school organizations were the

Altar boys from St. Hedwig 1921.Adolph Rucki, Krzeszowski, Meka, Rucki, Obizad—Owizarzark, Tadeuszak, Traczyk, Koniar—Kozlak, Murlowski, Tomczyk, Morytko, Lenart, Nowak—Wojciak, Nowak, Bochniak, Narog, Morytko, Zajac, Zawadzki—Koniar, Dambek, Tilas, Szsuaja—Horowicki, Daleki, Ptak, Kapala, Koscielniak, Stanowski, Kapala— Mikalski, Gawlik, Lopata, Maslowski—Balijewski, Nowak, Rolek—Morytko, Zawadzki, Handzel, Smykowski, Tomaszik, Reverand Father Cieminski, Father Worzala.

Choirgirls of St. Hedwig 1964.

Young Ladies' Sodality, Sacred Heart Society for Young Boys, Baseball Club, Girls Volleyball Club, Altar Boys, and Choir Girls (with annual Christmas caroling in the neighborhood). Vaudeville plays were put on every year to raise money for the school. These were popular events where the Polish White Eagle Band performed, directed by Mrs. Frank Shore and Mrs. John Zawislak. Everyone in the neighborhood attended. The school closed in 1969.

People from St. Hedwig attended the Eucharistic Congress in June of 1941.

St. Hedwig People at Eucharistic Congress, 1941.

St. Johns Lutheran Church first young peoples society. Miss Maier is the teacher in lower left hand corner 1890s.

ST. JOHN'S LUTHERAN GRADE SCHOOL
610 Northeast Broadway Avenue

In the 1860s, the St. John's congregation erected a school near Fourteenth Avenue and Main Street. A one-story parochial school was built when the church on Seventh and Main was erected. Later, this building was replaced with a two-story structure. The teacher for 1879, 1880, and 1881 was W. Gierke. In 1881, a fire in the home of Pastor Achilles destroyed the records of St. John's from 1867 to 1881. It is thought that the school closed in 1908 around the time that instruction was changed from German to English. German was then taught in the summer.

On September 3, 1975, the congregation decided to open a Christian Day School with 23 students. Miss Nancy Ehlert was the first teacher. A school bus was purchased and Robert Buschkopf became the second teacher and principal. Terry Schallert joined the staff in 1987. Kelley Schallert was added as a third teacher in 1988.

In 1990 a separate school building was purchased on 2101 Washington Street. Today there are 51 students from pre-kindergarten to eighth grade, taught by Barry Gostchock, Brenna Hollander, Nicole Sellick, and Ann Gutzke. The pastor and principal is the Reverend William J. Schaefer. The school secretary is Diane Hartwig. Mark Boyd is on the St. John's Board of Education. Although membership is now half what it was in the church's heyday, St. John's maintains a vital place in the community. When other churches left the city in the 1950s, 1960s, and 1970s, St. John's stayed.

St. John's Sunday school teachers of lower division 1967.

St. John's Lutheran School grades Pre K-5 on a field trip in the Fall of 2000.

Flames and smoke hid houses in crash area. Note parachute snagged in tree on left side.

7 Plane Crash on Memorial Day

Memorial Day 1957 started out as a typical holiday in Northeast Minneapolis. People were out on picnics, visiting cemeteries, fixing up their houses, and just plain relaxing. But when a jet plane thundered into the area of Pierce Street near Twentieth Avenue, the neighborhood turned into a scene of pandemonium. Blasts, explosions, strange objects falling from the sky, burning houses and cars, blaring sirens of fire trucks, and ambulances sent people screaming and running in all directions.[4]

Two planes had collided. They were part of a Navy squadron of four F9F Panther jets flying a Memorial Day salute to the war dead at Sunset Memorial Park Cemetery. The first plane crashed into a parked car in front of 1950 Pierce Street Northeast and set four houses on fire—at 1946, 1950, 1952, and 1958 Pierce Streets.

One pilot's body was thrown from his plane and landed in the street. John Terness, one of the many witnesses, said he moved the body out of the street and covered it. The pilot of the second plane ejected from his flaming aircraft and parachuted to safety, but his chute had to be cut from the trees in which it was tangled to rescue him. He landed on his feet, eleven blocks away from where the plane landed, at Nineteenth and Johnson Street. He was lucky enough to escape with only minor burns. At least nine people were injured but only one seriously, and no one on the ground died.

Rescue Equipment to the Scene

All available fire equipment was rushed to the scene of the crash. The blaze was brought under control in a short time. One airplane had dug a hole in front of 1950 Pierce Street, shoving a parked car up against a house and then demolishing the car and damaging two other cars as it bounced to a halt. Police, fire and newspaper switchboards were jammed with reports of airplane parts falling at various locations. Part of a wing and apparently a fuel tank fell at Twenty-second Street and Benjamin Avenues Northeast.

Most witnesses agreed that the two planes clipped wings during a rolling maneuver after the second pass had begun. Many said a wing was severed off the lead airplane, sending it into a steep dive. The second burst into flames, and moments later disintegrated in the air, strewing debris over an area of about one mile. The main portion fell in an open area at Fillmore Street and Sixteenth Avenue near Northeast Athletic Field, where 150 to 200 children were playing ball. Throughout the day, thousands of spectators watched debris being hauled away and asked a million questions about what happened as they stared at the blackened homes.

Northeast Neighbors Describe Crash

Four people in the **Herman Trost** residence at 1946 Pierce Street were in the basement of their home when they heard the explosions. When they smelled fumes and felt intense heat, they fled from the house and were not injured. The engine of the crashed plane struck in the back yard of the home across the alley. Mrs. Trost said she later found a 20-millimeter cannon from a plane in her living room.

Mr. and Mrs. Mike Swanson of 1958 Pierce Street said they were packing up a holiday picnic lunch when the crash occurred. When Mike heard his wife yell, "The house is on fire!" they panicked and began to throw some of their clothes out the upstairs windows. They were carrying heavy bundles outside, but when they realized what was happening, they dropped the bundles and ran to the assistance of their neighbors.

Anthony Sampson of 1927 Pierce Street Northeast, said. "I looked out the window in time to see the plane crash into some parked cars down the street and then several houses caught on fire." He tried to run toward the burning plane and houses, but he was cut off momentarily because flaming gasoline was "flowing in the gutter."

Mrs. Leon Burr of 1722 Northeast Pierce Street, was telling how at the time of the crash, she was frying eggs for the half-dozen members of her family who had accompanied her to her husband's and parent's graves. "The next thing I knew, I had rushed outside with the eggs in the frying pan still in my hand," she said. "The first things that came into my head was that the Russians were here."

Mrs. Eugene Peterson: "I saw a wing leave the plane and watched it land and the only thought that came to my mind was to follow that wing until I found my two children. As I left my yard I saw a little kid at Eighteenth and Fillmore turning in a fire alarm. He could hardly reach the box, so he jumped up and pulled the lever down, and I thought to myself, "What a smart kid.""

Aftermath

Commander Newell F. Olson, one of the pilots, known as "Big Ole," was killed. Big Ole flew on Thursday because he didn't want to ask any of his men to work on Memorial Day. The crew said he was that kind of guy. It was part of his job to procure services for groups who wanted flyovers on patriotic holidays. So he elected himself. He'd been around the hangar since early morning, after attending 6 o'clock Mass at St. Kevin's Catholic Church. How ironic that he was killed on a mission honoring the dead. There were no other fatalities from the crash, although General Hospital quickly mobilized for admissions of 25 people. John A. Forsmark, the second pilot, escaped with only minor burns. The Swanson home, at 1950 Pierce Street, was reportedly destroyed. The other three houses that took the brunt of the crash were heavily damaged.

[4]The information on the plane crash was taken from the Minneapolis Tribune and Minneapolis Journal accounts of the crash for May 30 and May 31, 1957.

8 Memory Lane – A Few Northeast Residents

Author's Note: I received letters from several people who wrote reminiscences about their days in Northeast Minneapolis, including Jim Cornish ("Redeye"), who now lives in Henderson, Nevada, and Jim Higgins, who lives in Columbia Heights. In addition, this section includes biographies of Doctor Edward and Doctor Leo Zaworksi, father and son, and Mrs. Ida Pudney's reminiscences of Northeast Minneapolis and the Maple Hill Sunday School.

The Zaworskis

For nearly 60 years Edward Zaworski and son Leo practiced medicine in Northeast Minneapolis, from 1917 to 1995. Most of those years were at Northeast Medical Clinic, 1229 Second Street Northeast

DOCTOR EDWARD ZAWORSKI

Edward Zaworski was born on a farm in Ashton, Nebraska, in a community of Polish people, a large number of whom eventually moved to Minneapolis, including Zaworski. He played baseball on a farm team in Ashton, Nebraska, and was catcher for Grover Alexander, who was later admitted to the Baseball Hall of Fame. He was also a thespian at Creighton University. He graduated from Creighton Medical School in

Edward Zaworski 1940s.

Omaha, and served as a medical officer in southern Minnesota during the flu epidemic during World War I.

Zaworski started his medical practice in 1917 at Seventeenth and Fourth Street Northeast in a building that housed Idzorek Drugstore, across from Holy Cross Church and Wines Department Store. He moved his office to Thirteenth and Second Street Northeast in 1928, making home visits to people who were unable to come to the office.

During the Depression he was often paid with eggs, chickens, or whatever people had. He drove as far as New Brighton, where a lot of Polish people who worked in the area lived. He would charge one dollar or two dollars per visit and dispensed medicine for free. People were poor in those days–pigeons were sometimes used for making soup. He once removed a patient's tonsils on the family's dining room table.

He liked the north woods. He and Stan Kapala often went to the lake together. He was very much involved in starting Polish-American groups like the Polish Boy Scouts, the Polish National Alliance, and the Polish White Eagles. He helped to develop *Nowiny Minnesota,* a Polish newspaper, with Joe Koleski. He was instrumental in starting St. Andrews Hospital in southeast Minneapolis, and was one of the first physicians at St. Mary's Hospital in Minneapolis.

He married Proxedes (Sadie) Gluba, and they had five children together: Raymond, a dentist; Francis, an art teacher; Edward, who worked for NSP; Margaret, a nurse; and Leo, an MD (see below). The family lived on Jefferson Street Northeast.

Leo Zaworski in his office the day of his retirement 1995.

DOCTOR LEO ZAWORSKI

Leo Zaworski followed in his father's footsteps, graduating from Marquette University in Milwaukee with a medical degree. He served as a medical officer in the Navy in World War II and the Korean War. He first started his private practice in the Polish White Eagle Building, which is kitty corner from the present clinic at Thirteenth and Second Street. How some patients climbed the stairs to the second floor is a wonder. He and Dr. Jack Kelly built the new medical clinic in the 1960s. He was known for his good sense of humor and his caring nature. He worked his whole life in Northeast Minneapolis and was well-loved by the people.

He was quite a jokester and prankster. He would plant fake vomit and then tell the nurses, "Clean up in room 3!" He would walk close to a car when the driver was pulling out, then grab his toes and say, "Oh, my gosh you ran over my foot!" If a child were in the office, he would say, "Oh, you're such a nice little girl," if it were a boy and the opposite if it were a girl, just to get them riled up. He had a pair of fake glasses with long nose and mustache to try to make the kids feel at ease.

He was very thoughtful and kind and used to pick up doughnuts for the nurses. Once after he retired, while he was on crutches from surgery, he picked up doughnuts at the Super America, and only later remembered that he had left his crutches on top of the gas pump. In bad weather, he would tell the women in the office to go home early and he would answer the phones. He was not really fluent in Polish, but knew enough phrases and could understand his patients. Some of the older patients would point to their ailments.

Many of the Northeast residents did not drive, so he would go on house calls at night; sometimes the rest of his family sat in the car while he was working. He never turned away patients even if they didn't have money. The clinic was open only until noon on Saturday, but the doctors and nurses were always there until 1 or 2 p.m. Once he went over to the receptionist's house and fixed her toilet. This was quite a kind deed, since he was not a handy man.

His daughter, Cindy, remembers her father stitching kids up on the kitchen table. There was a time when he gave more penicillin shots in the patients' bedrooms than he did at the clinic. Whenever he went back to visit the clinic after he retired, the patients were always happy to see him.

The Zaworski family couldn't go anywhere without someone recognizing him. Before long, they would be telling about their knee pains or other ailments in the parking lot. After he retired in 1995, he would say, "I have to go make my rounds." This meant he was going to visit people that were in the hospital or nursing homes. He even visited them at Christmas.

Some of the other doctors at the clinic were Doctors John Kelly, James Allen, John Salchet, Bruce O'Brien, Jim Lannon, Joseph Gasik, Jerry Heideman, and Dr. André. They sold the clinic to North Memorial in about 1994. Leo Zaworksi passed away in January of 2001.

Jim and Marilyn (Bubbles) Cornish
married 50 years 2001.

REDEYE (JIM CORNISH)

I am 72 years old and lived in Nordeast Minneapolis from about four to about fourteen years of age, but have some vivid memories.

We lived over the Ryola Bakery, which put out a bread similar to RyKrisp. In that row of buildings on the ground floor were the bakery, Kapala's Funeral Home, Mengelkoch's Hide and Tallow, the 101 Bar, a deserted theater, and Al's Texaco, where it was necessary to pump up the gas into a clear tank showing how many gallons were involved and then feed to the customer's car by gravity feed. I know, I helped Al when I was about five years old. Over the main course of the building stood the Germania Hall, which had been condemned for years and stood empty, I guess.

Our address was 1003 Northeast Main Street and the phone in Grandma Betz's apartment was Atlantic 5988. She and Grandpa Betz (Henry and Margaret, by name) had the larger of the two apartments over the Ryola bakery; they lived behind us and had the same address we did. On the corner of Main and Tenth Avenue Northeast was the Ryola Bakery; its address was 1001; upstairs from it was 1001 1/2, Hans Burmeister Upholstery. Across the hall and behind a metal fire door is where we lived at 1003 Northeast Main.

My stepfather, Leo M. Betz, was a good provider, since I know we were poor, but we did not lack for food or clothes as I recall. I remember the Carr-Cullen factory (makers of sashes and doors) down on Marshall Street. Past Broadway was the Grain Belt Brewery, on Marshall Street. I walked the two and a half blocks to school at Sheridan when E. A. Mooney was principal, and I believe his name was etched into the cornerstone. He was quite a man. I am probably prattling on, like a ship without a rudder, but it's kinda like being allowed to unload many thoughts, mostly good.

Down on the street level, next to the bakery was Kapala's Funeral Home, I believe, which was 1005 Main. They took up quite a bit of the building, but there was a driveway into the back yard, just beyond Mengelkoch's Hide and Tallow, which had many trucks. Between the burning of the hair from Kapala's and Mengelkoch's, we had quite a few smells over our back fence. We could see into that yard, and in fact, I would jump the fence and catch some of the wild kittens that lived back there, tame 'em, and turn them back.

Kapala's Funeral Home moved to near Second Street on Thirteenth Avenue. When it moved out, the

Anderson Chicken Company moved in below us and to the right. All those chickens, feathers, and whatever. The owner had a 1937 Ford coupe and didn't take very good care of its appearance. I talked him into letting me wash it a few times and he would pay me a dollar. Then I asked him one time if he wanted it waxed and he agreed. I got five dollars for that.

The 101 Bar was on the corner of Broadway and Main and was owned by the Sosneski family, who lived across the street from us. I got to know Matt, as he was just a bit older than I was. He eventually took over the bar, after the war [World War II], and I visited him there. Main Street was a very wide street and now has an island down the middle.

Tenth Avenue Northeast was only about three blocks long. It started at the Carr-Cullen plant and ran into a confluence of Broadway and University. This is where the Sheridan School was located. It was an interesting time for me and I believe that I was about 14 when we moved to south Minneapolis.

One of the first things I wanted as a kid was a flashlight and my stepdad told me to "earn it." I started by selling *Liberty* magazines for a nickel. I earned a cent and a half for each one. I built up quite a route and made enough to buy a used bicycle for $15.

Across the drive at Mengelkoch's was a bar called the 1013 Bar and I believe the Sosnieski family who owned the 101 Bar at Broadway and Main Northeast also owned it. Across the street from the 1013 Bar was Burkhardt's Plumbing and to the right of it was a row of houses built together. I guess you would call them tenements.

I believe the RyKrisp Company bought out the Ryola Company when Guy Fredin died and his son did not want to handle the firm. The Germania Hall was always a mystery to me since it was a very tall building with many floors and was condemned per the info given us kids. I wanted to go up there and look through it but never did. Never heard of the Main Street Theater, but there was one that was abandoned and wide open just short of Broadway and us kids would play in there once in a while. Right next to that and on the corner was Al's Texaco.

–Jim Cornish (Redeye) of Henderson, Nevada. This came from a series of letters to the author in September 2000. Cornish is called Redeye because he had a boat on the St. Croix River in Prescott, Wisconsin and his nickname was Cap'n Redeye.

JIM HIGGINS

My parents, James A. Higgins and Emma Amanda Ienfeldt, were married in Menomonee, Wisconsin, where my mother was from. In those days the mother often returned home to be near the family during the birth of a child. So I was born in Menomonee even though we lived in a small apartment in Minneapolis at the time. We lived in several different homes in Northeast, but primarily we lived at 918 Lowry Avenue, just off of Central. It was a four-plex behind the Arcana Masonic Temple Building. The house is not there any more.

My father was an upholsterer, but most of the time he worked for the Ford Motor Company on the assembly line, until they closed down when he was 50 years old in 1928. They closed down when a new model was introduced and he never got called back because he was too old. The plant was located near Fort Snelling. During the Depression, he worked for the WPA [Works Projects Administration] doing road construction and things of that nature. These were tough times, but everyone was in the same boat.

We had eight children in our family, five girls and three boys. A cousin of mine from Menomonee named Kenny Webster moved up here because he couldn't find any work. He lived with us for about six to eight months until he was able to find a job and an apartment. I would put up a folding cot every night in the kitchen. My brother slept on a cot, too. My sisters were on the davenport in the living room, or they had some roll-a-way. We would put these out at night and store them away in the morning. We all ate together in the dining room. It made for a close-knit family.

We had a good time even though there were many things we had to do without. We had good neighbors and the kids all played together. Friends were your lifelines. You spent a lot of time with them because there was nothing else to go to. Nobody had a car. My dad never had a car in his whole life. The only car we ever had was when I bought myself a new 1941 Plymouth four-door sedan.

We didn't have a backyard to play in. So we played out in the yard behind the buildings on Central Avenue. Between the alley and the buildings there was nothing but dirt. We played ball and Ante, Ante Over. We sometimes played golf with a boy named Clayton. His dad owned the Thurston Shoe Store. At that time, golf was just coming out [in our neighborhood]. Clayton had a couple of golf clubs and balls. He dug a few holes and we'd play, until his dad would come and tell him to leave those little boys alone and come in and go to work. Another one of our neighbor's dads worked for the Pillsbury Company. Every night we would go over to their place and play Hearts. They would have a great big dishpan of popcorn that we all shared.

I started going to the Y when I was about 10 or 12 years old at Twenty-fourth and Central, which was a block away from us. But there were no organized sports through the parks. The only time I went down to the Neighborhood House was when I was a little older and learned how to dance. And there was a swimming pool down at John Ryan's on East Hennepin. But my folks never allowed us to go where there was any water. They were deathly afraid of water. My dad had an experience when he was out east in a boys' home. They threw him in the water. After the third time he went down, some brother jumped in and retrieved him. My mother was always afraid, too. Neither of them knew how to swim.

I attended Prescott Elementary, then Edison High School and graduated in 1935.

When I was going to Edison we had 20 minutes to eat so I went home for lunch. My mother always had a meal for me. Parents and authorities were a little stricter than they are now. You had to adhere to the curfews or else. You couldn't wander around during school hours the way they do now.

One of the first jobs my older sister and I had was at a face powder business. We would be there at nighttime, filling small boxes with face powder. You had to do it by hand with a teaspoon. We inhaled an awful lot of powder. There was a blacksmith shop on Lowry, just west of the four-plex unit we lived in. We spent a lot of time just watching the horses and smelling the hoofs getting burnt.

In the beginning, Lowry Avenue was all residential. It wasn't until later years that they had some industry come in. There were two grocery stores between Central and Taylor. They all made a living even though they were located in the same area. People who lived in the community owned all the drugstores and butcher shops. We did our grocery shopping at the store that was in the Masonic Temple building right next to us. You could charge groceries in those days. Some of the grocery stores that were on Central Avenue during the 40s and 50s were Eck and Anderson's Red and White, Hart's, Maas Grocery, and Larson's, who [members of this family] later became doctors. There were also a lot of meat markets like Fagerof, Wachsmuth, Al Strandine's, and Cataract Meats.

I used to hang around the men's furnishing store on Lowry and Central after school and Saturdays. It was called Katin's Haberdashery. I would work there right before Christmas and for Jewish holidays. And then before I graduated, I was working there quite a bit of the time because they had a new owner who couldn't afford the full salary of the fellow who was employed there. So he asked me if I would care to work. So when I was through with school, I started working there. Little by little, business got better and I was able to work my way in. My boss was a fellow named Sam Katin from Dassel, Minnesota. I worked for Sam for 19 years.

I was selling insurance part-time when I was working in men's furnishings. It started in 1940. Two fellows came in and wanted to know if I would be interested in writing insurance. And I said yes. A friend of mine, Ralph Stein, was a banker at Central Northwestern Bank. His brother, Ed Stein, was in the insurance business. So I started selling life insurance with him. And when Ed passed away, Ralph talked me into buying Ed's business. It was a small agency, and I bought it in 1946. I had quite a bit of business built up working in the store with the customers that came in. And the Jewish fellow that I worked for was supportive. As a matter of fact I was writing part of his insurance.

My first loyalty was to the store where I worked. And that's what Sam Katin said: "Well, when I need him he is here. What he does on his own, that's his business. More power to him." Sam was a wonderful guy.

On July 1, 1950, I bought my first agency on Nineteenth and Central Avenue. I left the store then. As an independent agent, you could own your own business. I made a lot of friends in men's furnishings. And a lot of these folks became policyholders of mine.

There were changes after the war when I got back. In about 1955 on Central Avenue they tried to get a large supermarket and department store in. There was just no way. When the shopping centers did come in, why that kind of took away a lot of the local merchants. And then too, new developments sprung up. People wanted to move up to the other side of Johnson Street. St. Anthony and Columbia Heights expanded. The community wasn't as stable as it used to be.

I put up the down payment for the last home that my folks had on 2614 Polk Street. I was working then and living at home. The house was well built. It had four bedrooms and a beautiful porch in front. My mother enjoyed sitting out there and watching all the neighbors go by.

I married my wife in 1945. Her name is Clara Buchinger and she was born on Twenty-sixth and Grand Street. We were neighbors and also went to the same church, which was St. Paul's Lutheran. We went together for about eight years. I didn't think I could afford to get married. I figured I had to work for a while. Her father had a business on Twenty-sixth Avenue called Buchinger Funeral Home. Clara passed away in November of 2000. We were married for 55 years and have three children: Jim Higgins, Darlene Higgins, and Marilyn Higgins Pavlak. We also have four grandsons.

Jim Higgins and his wife Clara, when Jim was 1989 Grand Marshall of the Eastside Parade.

—*Jim Higgins, excerpts taken from Life History Interviews by Harley Schreck, Ph.D., Bethel College in St. Paul, December 15, and February 14, 1994. Copies of the interview are in possession of the author.*

Girlhood Memories of Maple Hill Sunday School

By Mrs. Ida M. Pudney

I was born in 1885 near the tracks in the lower Northeast area. This was the old St. Paul and Southern Railroad line that had a spur track going to Hinckley. One day, I saw the charred train with its smashed windows that had carried the victims from the terrible 1894 Hinckley fire. Through the black darkness of the shattered windows, I remember thinking that I could see these sorry victims as they moved slowly past like a funeral procession. Across these tracks I would go every Sunday to the Maple Hill Sunday School, sometimes when it was bitterly cold.[5,6]

The Sunday school was conducted by Charles M. Way and would always begin with prayer. I remember sitting on long unfinished planks supported by cordwood that looked like tree stumps. The benches had no backs and made us sit up straight. I particularly remember how the pastor's wife, Mrs. Stevens, would parade in front of us with her huge apron filled with some imaginary objects. One day she said that it was filled with kittens and really made us all giggle and laugh when she quickly opened the apron and let them fall to the ground. It was always a big surprise because I think we all wanted to believe that the apron was filled with kittens.

After prayer, we would always hold a singing contest. All of the youngsters would line up and walk past the penny box singing "Listen to the pennies drop, listen to the pennies fall, everyone for Jesus, he will receive them all." All of us were very poor, but we all had our penny for the penny box.

When I was about eight years old, I remember 200 men from Coxey's army up here, tired, hungry and looking for jobs. The Sunday school set up tables along old Division Street (now Central Avenue) and neighbors from all around brought food to feed them. I still wonder why their blue uniforms did not look like regular military uniforms.[7]

As a child, I used to walk papa to work every morning and meet him every night. He was a millwright. It was always lots of fun because papa would tell me a new story or have a new ribbon or candy stick for me. I remember how he would bring us fresh, cool water from the neighborhood well–it tasted better than anything else. For washing water, Papa would carry the water in buckets with a yoke from the cooper shop

5 This information was originally published in the *East Side Argus*, October 31, 1963.

6 The Hinckley Forest Fire on September 1, 1894, was a "a hurricane of fire swept from nearby forests into Hinckley and the town was destroyed," writes Theodore Blegen in *Minnesota: A History of the State*. A train managed to get out with 276 men, women, and children in a dramatic rescue by the engineer, but 197 died in the Hinckley fire.

Northeast Sunday School Class Of 1890

1890 class of Maple Hill Sunday School at 600 NE Fillmore.

across the street. We would never drink the water, but it was good for washing. I think they used it for sealing the barrels.

I was 17 before I was allowed out on the street after seven o'clock. And then I had to be home by half past nine. The sidewalk in front of our house on Division Street was made of wood and was cracked and filled with holes where the boards had been removed. My folks were afraid that I would hurt myself on the sidewalk. If we went anywhere at night, even next door, we went as a family.

I remember one day when I was skipping rope that one of the Sunday school teachers was watching me. He came up to me and said, "Tootsie, you are going straight to hell." I was so frightened that I ran home crying. Papa comforted me and explained that some of the church people were pretty radical. I look back and think that I was so fortunate to live in a family with so much love and understanding.

Today, I wonder what has happened to our children. Parents don't spend any time with their kids; they don't show them any discipline, and I can't see where the kids are very happy. In my day, we kids did what we were told and we respected our folks for their judgment. Back then, we knew what it was to love your folks and your neighbors-we worked together, laughed together and loved one another. I don't see this love today.

In 1893, our Sunday school was turned into Pierce School. For seven years they used this building until the new Pierce School was built in 1900. After that, the building was sold to a man who turned it into a six-plex.

These are some of the girlhood memories of an old lady. Things have changed so much today and so few of the people from that time are left that all I have left is the one photo of Maple Hill Sunday School and many, many memories. That photo is now my whole life. Sometimes, when I pick it up and see my sister near the railing on the left or the pastor and his wife in the middle, I think I can hear the singing of "listen to the pennies drop." Or see them huddled together on the long hard benches. In my heart, the Maple Hill Sunday School is still there on Fillmore Street.

---

[7] "Coxey's Army" was only one of a number of groups of unemployed men who formed "armies" during the Depression of 1893-94. The armies called upon the unemployed to march upon Washington and deliver demands for relief to Congress. This most famous army was led by Populist Jacob S. Coxey of Ohio.

Snapshots

and

Vignettes

A still on University Avenue that was raided by John Belair and the Purity Squad in 1929.

Friends of Margaret Moerls
(Aka Buttons)

Grain Belt fishing trip

Band from St. Mary's Russian Orthodox Church in 1910

Soo Line Railroad people at a picnic in 1905.

Central Avenue Parade May 30, 1919.

Soo Line Workers.

Jacob Schnitzius Cooperage Plant at 72 Eighth Street NE in 1880.

Mike Deutscher is mounted policeman in St. Anthony, 1870s

Dee Lunblad Abrahamson, Barbara Ness Little, Madonna Floyd Spechts, Kae Elhke Noren on Easter Sunday 1940s.

The cashier's cage during a robbery at the Minneapolis Brewing Company in 1941. A man was killed by a ricocheted bullet.

Contest at Theilman's Drugstore at Lowry and Second Street NE in 1930s.

Graco Employee Picnic 1931

Northern States Power Company's third annual picnic in 1912.

Lagerquist and Son's Foundry at 13th Avenue and Water Street NE in 1926.

Ladies from Polanie Club demonstrating Wycinanki
(Polish paper cutting) at the Festival of Nations.

Ready Meats 1970-Dan Ready, Cliff Carlson, Arnie Carlson,
George Shimshock, and Bill Howell.

Edith Cavell School 1949.

Joe Kapala dresses up for Popravinie, Polish and Slovak custom where couple is serenaded the day after the wedding with pots and pans, 1940s.

This was a community pump where people gathered, located on 10th and Marshall Street, 1920s.

Minneapolis Ice Company distributed ice in Northeast Minneapolis. It was owned by Roy Hall and F. Palmer, 1905.

10 Sports

A group from the Sokols club, a Slovak organization that promotes young athletes.

Northeast Women's League at Central Avenue Bowling Alleys 1930s.

General Mills Team, 1940s.

Schiller lads again win title and Tribune award in 1932. They defeated Seward in the baseball finals at Nicollet Park From left-Coach John Deno, Ed Ziviaska, Frank Duda, Frank Trachek, Ed Drabczak, Ed Kondzilski, John Wojciak, Walter Wolinski, Paul Loch, Mike Jarosak, Stanley Fudro and William Warhol. In front is Frank Wolinski, mascot.

Captain Steve Vanusek accepts the city grade school basketball trophy for Schiller in 1931.

Louis Lopata earned six letters in three sports while attending Edison High in the 1920s. He then taught at Sheridan before moving to Edison as Pete Guzy's assistant football coach in 1941 and retired in 1962. He led the teams on to many victories.

A determined Joe Holewa dribbles downcourt at a University of Minnesota game against Michigan 1948.

Joe Sodd looking at his score card with Pat Sawyer. He graduated from Edison in 1947-48 and went on to become a professional golfer.

Northwestern Telephone Exchange Company on Central Avenue, early 1900s.

Our Lady of Lourdes Orioles basketball team park board champs 1928. Front row-Henri Emond, Clarence Durand, George Belair, Earl Carpentier. Middle row-unk. Carl Bolander, Harold Fischer, unk, unk. Top row- unk, Leo Marcotte, Henry Columbe, unk, unk, unk, Ernest Abraham.

Bottineau Park Baseball City Champs in 1925.

Jersey Ice Cream Football team 1930s.

Baseball team sponsored by the B and B Bar, 1940s.

Clayton Tonnamaker graduated from Edison in 1948 and went on to play for the Green Bay Packers.

Zig Bishop coached baseball team in 1930s.

Bottineau Football Team of 13 year olds in 1947. 1st row-Rich Lubinski, unk, Andy Zurbey, Joe Zych, Bill Kozlak, Jerry Pierce, Tom Stawski, unk, 2nd row-Ron Barrett, Dick Sappa, unk, unk, Ray Kocon, Dick Stowski, Ernie Birch, 3rd row-Head coach, John Sichak, Bill Kennedy, unk, Chuck Allsion, Dick Alberico, Firman Janski, Tom Reynolds, Assistant coach Ted Partyka.

Top Row—Stevens, Johnson, Malloy, Nelson, Mr. Hendricks, Berg, Peterson, Nordin, Olson
Front Row—Feeney, Larson, Sporre, Thies, Peterson, Kauth

Bowling team sponsored by the B and B Bar.

HOCKEY

THE hockey team had its most successful finish in the season of 1925-26. This was accomplished by combining Mr. Hendricks' coaching ability with the hard work of the squad. The only loss recorded against the Tommies was the championship game and thus Edison holds second place. Although the title was not won, the team built a reputation of having strong offensive and defensive playing strength at their call. The team showed great fighting spirit and fair sportsmanship in all the games.

The hockey squad of this season was one of the largest and strongest ever representing Edison. Two of the players, Captain Olson and "Jim" Feeney won berths on the all-city hockey sextet. Clarence Sporre won honorable mention for his steady and dependable playing.

The squad will suffer the loss of a number of lettermen for the next hockey season. Four members of the 1925-26 team graduate in June. They are Captain Orville Olson, Hubert Nelson, Delbur Nordin, and Floyd Moloy.

Clarence Sporre was elected to captain the 1926-27 hockey team. The next season's squad will be lighter, but all members are fast skaters and will make a good showing.

ORVILLE OLSON

Zig Bishop, Steve Bishop, Joe Dudjac, Hank Bishop, 1935.

25-Year Anniversary of the Goldbrick Team taken in 1979. Pete Warian, Leonard Borgstrom, Steve Fellegy, Tom Fellegy, Paul Zurbey, George Hauck, Mike Sodd, Vern Kuduk, Duane Haas, Norman Gallus, Rich Podany. Celebrated at Jax CafÈ, band in the background is Joe Glowacki and the Northeast Five, they sang all in Polish. The Gold Brick Club was formed in 1947. They were a group of kids that hung around the Nuthouse (Northeast Neighborhood House). Many of them were in trouble. Some of the team names were Termites, Allies, Kleptoes, Rainbows, Schwishers, Shamrocks, and St. Mary's Vets.

Zurbey's Girls Softball team 1989. Top row-Sue Johnson, Barb Carla, Marlene Ward, Karen Kostik, Georgie Zurek, Roxana Zurek, Paula Haynes. Bottom row-Cheryl Zurek, Julie Jaslyn, Chris, Jill Nitke, Julieanne Crossman, Lori Meyer.

218

Girl's Softball Team 1939 1st Row–Margaret Johnson, Elvira Gronberg, Gladys Pendzimaz, Irene Schultz Willson, Mary Masica, Gen Groetchil Back Row–Betty-O'Shea, Helen Kluk, Meryl Gilbertson, Stan Peterson, Marie L, Vi Grabski, Marge Frenzel.

Gymnasts of St. Veronica's Wreath from St. Cyril's Church competing at the National Meet in 1939.

Ma Curry. She looked like a thermometer on a hot day. She was tall and slender and often wore red dresses. She taught at Pillsbury Grade School in the 1920s and in 1929 she moved to Edison High School, where she taught Civics for the next thirty years. During the Depression she bought clothes and breakfast for anyone in need. She sensed that through participation in sports, good men with little hope in the future could learn to be winners in life. She kept dozens of young boys in school with her friendship and encouragement. The 1937 basketball team that won the state tournament rode to the game in Ma Curry's car. She also took them out for malts after every game. After the boys graduated she went on to become friends with their wives, children and grandchildren. During World War II she wrote regularly to every boy who wrote to her. When the number reached 125 she started publishing a weekly newsletter. She had no children of her own. But she was part mother to hundreds.

1899 Island Cycle Supply sponsored baseball team of Swandberg and Anderson, which later became Swandberg and Scheefe.

Central Avenue Men's Bowling League, some of the sponsors were Huddle Bar, Zip Bottling Co., Joe's Barber Shop, Vilhella Brothers Beverage Co., and the B and B Bar. 1930s.

Bibliography

From Mansions to Quonset Huts

Anderson, Mike, "Northeast Heritage Beyond the Grain Belt," *Northeaster,* March 23, 1998.

Baas, Jeff. "The McMillan-Lacy-Bros Mansion," (unpublished manuscript, 1994).

Baas, Jeff and Garden District Club *Historic Garden District Gazette,* March 25, 1993 and May 1993.

Baldwin, Robert F. "Roomers, and Truth: Boardinghouses Said 'Welcome Home' to Generations of Farmhands and Office Clerks as They Ventured out in Search of Careers and Adventures," *Country Home,* May/June 1997.

Dean, Patty, "It is Here We Live," *Minnesota History,* 57 (Spring 2001): 5.

"Doomed House Has History—May Be First One Built in City," *Minneapolis Star,* May 17, 1963.

"German-Born Eastsider Pursues Hobby of Making His Home Surroundings Unique," *Minneapolis Argus,* October 15, 1968.

Hanneman, Doug, "Remember When? Quonset Huts Offered Temporary Housing."

Johnson, Walter, "Is the Godfrey House Oldest in City? Two Other Homes Were Built in 1848," *Minneapolis Star,* January 2, 1952.

Keaveny, Joan, "Quonset Homes," *Minneapolis Tribune,* November 27, 1949.

Koop, Peggy M., "Minneapolis Bed and Breakfast Offers City and Victorian Decor," *Minneapolis Star Tribune,* September 13, 1990.

Lamb, Lynette, "Bountiful Bed and Breakfasts [LeBlanc House]," *Mpls/St. Paul,* August 1993.

LeBlanc House *see LeBlancHouse.com,* Internet site.

"St. Anthony Renewal Stirs Emotion," *Minneapolis Tribune,* April 15, 1974.

Zellie, Carole, and Gameth O. Peterson, *Northeast Minneapolis Historic Context Study* (Minneapolis Heritage Preservation Commission and The Minneapolis Planning Department, 1998).

Connections

Anderson, Mike, "At Birth of Art-A-Whirl, Organizing Artists Was Like ' "Herding Cats,'" *Northeaster,* May 16, 2000.

Northeast Minneapolis Arts Association, *Art-A-Whirl,* May 18, 2001.

Ashmore, Kerry, "Naming Shopping Center 'The Quarry' Won't Begin to Tell the History of Northeast's Stone Crushing," *Northeaster,* January 29, 1996.

Becera, Marilyn, "Step into Wines Department Store—and Back a Few Decades," *Minneapolis Star Tribune,* July 7, 1974.

Behrens, Shirley, "Last of 'Ma and Pa' Groceries Closes 45 Years of Serving Northeast Neighborhood," *Northeast Sun,* [n.d.] 1973, in Hennepin County History Center clipping files.

"Dreblow Tells of Gamble's History," *Minnetonka Record,* November 17, 1949.

"Eastside Rich in Stone and Brick," *Minneapolis Journal,* March 29, 1914.

Ethnic Dance Theatre, see *Internet site: ethnicdancetheatre.com* (Joan Elwell, webmaster).

Flanagan, Barbara, "There Goes . . . the Old Neighborhood," *Minneapolis Star,* February 19, 1970.

Fortman, Gwendolyn, "The High Cost of Progress," *Minneapolis Star Tribune,* [n.d.] 1999. Copy in possession of author.

Fuehrer, Tim, "Dangerous Abandoned Pits Claimed Several Lives," *Northeaster,* October 17, 1990.

Fuller, Jim, "An Edgewater Inn Tradition Comes Kicking Back to Life," *Minneapolis Star Tribune,* September 7, 1984.

"Gamble Skogmo Story," *Sun Newspapers,* November 27, 1968.

"Gamble Stores—Minneapolis Industries," *Minneapolis Journal,* April 26, 1935.

Gelbach, Deborah L. *From This Land: A History of Minnesota's Empires, Enterprises.* Northridge, CA: Windsor Publications, 1988.

Graco Story 75th Anniversary 1926-2001 (Minneapolis, 2001).

Graco The First 50 Years and the Next 50 Years Annual Report, 1976.

Graco Inc.see *Internet site: graco.com.*

"Hamburger Joint Seeks Northeast Memorabilia," *Minneapolis Argus,* December 13, 1978.

"History of Franklin Manufacturing Company, 1935-1975," [n.d]., unpublished manuscript, in possession of author.

Iggers, Jeremy, "Gasthof Has Vitality and It's Fun," *Minneapolis Star Tribune,* December 11, 1992.

Ingman, Harvey, "Grand New Center Marks Gamble Skogmo Growth," *Minneapolis Tribune,* February 15, 1948.

Jones, Will, "Real Onion Rings Do Exist," *Minneapolis Star Tribune* [n.d.]. Copy in Hennepin County History Center clipping file.

K. W., "Arthur's: The Great Onion Ring Legend," *Sun Weekender,* August 18, 1978. Copy in Hennepin County History Center clipping file.

Martin, Virginia L., "At the Murphey Mom and Pop," *Hennepin History* 51 (Fall 1992): 24-31.

Mason, Ralph "Gamble-Skogmo Acquires Control of Western Auto," *Minneapolis Star,* August 6, 1958.

Meyer, Jim, "A Brave Combo: Polka and Pop at Mario's," *Minneapolis Star Tribune,* July 5, 1996.

"Movie Theater is Wrecked by Bomb Explosion," *Minneapolis Star Tribune,* May 19, 1926.

"New Gamble Store Opened," *Minneapolis Tribune,* August 18, 1939.

"New Store Opens on Central Avenue [Gambles]," *Minneapolis Tribune,* March 12, 1937.

"Northeast Minneapolis Grocer George Zahuranec Quitting after 40 Years of Business," *Minneapolis Tribune,* September 16, 1977.

Olson, Gail, "Professional Ethnic Dance Company Likes Northeast's Cultural Mix," *Northeaster,* November 2, 1998.

—"Rhythmland Roller Rink to Close Soon," Northeaster, June 19, 2001.

—"Edgewater Eight Will Reunite For a Concert at Orchestra Hall," *Northeaster,* March 23, 1998.

—"Old Quarry Swimmin' Hole had History of Accidents," *Northeaster,* February 23, 1998.

Parker, Melissa, "Pitter Patter," *Skyway News,* July 26, 1977.

Phantom Diner's Twin Cities Restaurant Guide (Minneapolis: Waldman House Press, 1985).

Quarry, several articles on, 1920-1936 in Minneapolis Public Library Special Collections.

"Red Asplund Will Be Grand Marshall, East Side Parade," *Northeaster,* July 20, 1995.

Serum, Kristin, "Old Northeast Gang Will Honor Cafe Owners," *Minneapolis Star,* January 28, 1967.

Smith, G. Hubert, "Minnesota Potteries: From Pioneer Craft to Modern Factory," *Minnesota History* 33 (Summer 1953): 229-235.

Wasie Foundation Scholarship see *Internet Site: interact.ru/foundation/main.htm.*

Wickland, John, "Gambles Sells Its Chain of Food Stores," *Minneapolis Tribune,* December 17, 1950.

Wood, Dave, "Latvian Tailor Outwears Life's Tougher Fabrics," *Minneapolis Star Tribune,* October 1, 1983.

Author interviews starting in June 2000 to June 2001 with Mike Abrahamovitz, Gary Burkhardt, Dominic and Kathy Castino, Jim Brown, Jim Dusenka, Joan Elwell, Jimmy Harris, Joe Holewa. Leo Kiefer, John Kremer, Bob Lohmar, Al Morelli, Thom Markley, Charles Murlowski, Robert Schroeder, Gordon Solz, and Joan Turpin, Notes in possession of author.

Author interviews at Rhythmland on June 30, 2001 with Ron Benson, Carol Boyda, Carolyn Gage, Don and Peggy Gese, Bill Gese, Karen Haverty and Bonnie Iacarella, Evelyn Wilson, Notes in possession of author.

Parks, Playgrounds, and Pageants

Ashmore, Kerry, "Logan Park was Northeast's 'Melting Pot' Earlier in the 20th Century," *Northeaster,* April 17, 1995.

—"After 30 Years on the Northeast Parks Beat, a 'Copper' Gets Well Known," *Northeaster,* December 21, 1994.

Flanagan, Barbara, "Songs to Be Sent via Tape Recording," *Minneapolis Tribune,* August 6, 1952.

Judge, Gillian, "Young Yardville," *Hennepin History* 49:3 [Summer 1990] 4-11.

Lagemann, John Kord, "Leave It to the Kids!" *McCall's,* October 1950.

Linders, Carol, "Community Sings, Band Concerts Colored Windom Park's First 100 Years," *Northeaster,* May 20, 1987.

Logan Park playbills and newspaper clippings, 1920-1932 from Claire Burgoyne and Carol Paquette.

Olson, Gail, "Parks Reflect Northeast History, People," *Northeaster,* October 9, 1999.

—"Some Northeast Parks Honor War Heroes," *Northeaster,* November 18, 1999.

Van Ruden, John, articles from various newspapers, including *Minneapolis Journal,* 1940s to 1956, and *East Minneapolis Argus,* October 30,1952, all in possession of Irene Van Ruden Trench.

Author interviews with Claire Burgoyne and Carol Paquette, May 2001. Notes in possession of author.

Cemeteries, Gravestones and Funeral Chapels

"Beltrami Park Gravestones Tell a Historical Tale," *Minneapolis Star Tribune* (Fixit) May 28, 1989.

Blomfield, E. A. Cemeteries, *Hillside, Sunset, and St. Anthony,* 1936, in clipping files Minneapolis Public Library Special Collections.

Graves, Chris, "Vandalism in Catholic Cemetery on Holy Day Suggests Satanism," *Minneapolis Argus,* May 15, 1995.

St. Anthony of Padua Cemetery, 1851-1995 (Roseville, MN: Park Genealogical Books 1999).

Strom, Judy Anne, "Tombstones: Silent History Lesson," *Minneapolis Argus,* July 5, 1972.

Author interviews with Tom Glodek, Ed Rainville, Roy Hunt, and Bill McReavy, Sr., October 2001. Notes in possession of author.

Parochial Schools

Church of St. Charles Borromeo, 1938-1963: 25 Years of Growth (Minneapolis, 1963).

Church of St. Cyril: 90th Anniversary (Minneapolis, 1981).

De La Salle High School 100th Anniversary, May 7, 2000 (Minneapolis, 2000).

De La Salle brochure (Minneapolis, n.d.).

Church of All Saints, Golden Jubilee, 1916-1966, August 21, 1966.

Haidet, Mark and Kathryn Haidet with Melissa Salisbury and Jubilee Committee, *St. Charles Borromeo 50th Anniversary* (Minneapolis, 1988).

"Invitation: Say Goodbye to 1914 St. Anthony School," *Northeaster,* May 29, 1982.

Johnson, Kay, *History of De La Salle, 75th Anniversary* (Minneapolis, 1975).

Kinney, John F., *Souvenir of the Blessing of All Saints Parish Center,* November 1, 1979.

Morris, Margaret, "School Addition to be Dedicated in St. Anthony," May 13, 1960.

Notre Dame De Minneapolis—The French-Canadian Catholics. (Minneapolis: Our Lady of Lourdes Parish, 1977).

Olson, Gail, "De La Salle High: A Century of Change, From Vocational School to College Prep" *Northeaster,* February 22, 2000.

One Hundred Years: The Centennial History of St. Boniface, 1858-1958 (Minneapolis: 1958).

St. Charles 40th Anniversary, 1938-1978 (Minneapolis, 1978).

St. Cyril's Church Centennial, Commemorative Book (Minneapolis, 1991).

St. John's 125th Anniversary, 1867-1992. (Minneapolis, 1992).

St. John's Evangelical Lutheran Church Centennial, 1867-1967 (Minneapolis, 1967).

Author interview with Corinne Diffley, Janice Carroll, Margaret Hoben, and Alice Rainville November 2001. Notes in possession of author.

People and Events

Burke, Evelyn. "Wayzata's Marie Wasie Loves Polish Scholars," *Wayzata-Plymouth Sailor,* August 13, 1984.

Kleeman, Richard P., "I Thought the Russians Were Here," *Minneapolis Tribune* May 31, 1957.

Magnuson, Ed, "Quiet Day Explodes in a Flaming Crash," *Minneapolis Tribune* May 31, 1957.

Romer, Sam, "Second Navy Pilot Parachutes Safely in Crash Over City," *Minneapolis Tribune* May 31, 1957.

Author phone interviews and letters of Jerome Choromanski, October 2001. Notes in possession of author.

Author interviews through letters with "Redeye,"-Jim Cornish, September 2000, Jim Higgins courtesy of interviews by Harley Schreck, PhD, Bethel College December 15 and February 14, 1994, phone interviews with Cindy Spear and Frances Zaworski August 2001, and "Maple Hill Sunday School" by Ida M. Pudney, *East Side Argus* October 31, 1963, printed with permission of William Pudney. Notes in possession of author.

Photo Credits

Ruth Jurisch, photographer 12

Doug Kieley, photographer 24 R, 31 L&R, B, 32, 33 U&L, 36 L&R, 37, 38, 39 L&R, 41 U, L& R, 42, 48, 54, 58, 60, 80, 84, 87,91 L, 108 R

LuAnn Golen, photographer 140, 141 L, R, B, 142 L&R, 143 L&R

Minnesota Historical Society 22, 24 L, 26, 30; Philip C. Dittes, 31 B, 33; Minneapolis Star Journal, 38, 39 L&R, 42, 48, 84, 91; Daniels Studio, 108; Minneapolis Journal, 112, 146, 148, 197 L & B, 198, 199, 203 U&B, 204; Charles J. Hibbard

Minnesota Transportation Museum 24

Minneapolis Public Library, Minneapolis Collection 29, 88 U&R, 106, 109, 180, 192, 201

Hennepin County History Center 30 R, 34, 43, 44, 85, 120, 121, 122 U&B, 123, 124.125L, 126, 129 R, 206

Minneapolis Parkboard Archives 107, 108 L, 110 U&L, 111 L, R, B, 113 L, 114, 115 L&R, 116, 132, 134

"A Golden Pastorate," 1964 Church of St. Hedwig's Golden Jubilee Booklet 177

All Saints 1975 Parish Booklet and 1966 Golden Jubilee Book 150, 151

Church of Holy Cross Centennial 1986 Booklet 152, 153, 154, 155 L&R, B, BR

Church of St. Cyril Golden Jubilee 1941 Booklet 174, 175 L&R, U, 219 BL

Edison Wizard Yearbook 1963, 1946, 1926, 1945 -210 U, 214, 219, 139

St. Anthony Yearbook 1947 Anthonian 160, 161

Story of a Hundred Years-St. Anthony of Padua 163 U&B

St. Charles Borromeo School 170, 171, 172, 173

St. John's Lutheran School 178, 179 U&B

Gary/Josie Kvistberg 13, 14

Author's Family Collection 15, 16, 17, 18, 19, 20 L&R, 45, 177 R&L

Phyllis Askay 27, 95 L&R, 216, Cover

Marsha Carlson 34

Sun Weekender 43, 44 Aug. 18, 1978

Eastside Argus 40, 52, 98, 99, 100,101 December 1, 1971, September 6, 1940, April 26, 1972

Gasthof zur Gemutlichkeit 44 R

Janice Carroll 46 L&R, 208, 214, 216 U, 221

Lloyd Bergman 47 L&R

Dominic Castino 50

Jim Dusenka 53

Joan Elwell 55, 56

Gary Gese 62, 63 L&R

Caroline Gage 65, 66, 68, 69

Chris Burkhardt 70, 71 L

Leo Kiefer 71, 72, 73

Bob Lohmar 74

Index

About the Author

Genny Kieley is the author of three books about Northeast Minneapolis. She meets regularly with a group called Local Writers in Maple Grove and is currently working on a collection of stories that are based on true-life experiences. They are laced with the poignancy and humor of life. She also plans to finish a historical novel based on farm life in the 1940s. She dreams of traveling to Poland and standing on the land where her grandparents lived. She feels this will enrich her writing about Polish immigrants and their struggle of leaving their homeland. Her other interests include decorating, gardening and spending time with her grandchildren.